THE AMERICAN SPIRIT

THE PAINTINGS OF MORT KÜNSTLER

TEXT BY HENRY STEELE COMMAGER

EPILOGUE BY ROD GRAGG

BIOGRAPHY BY M. STEPHEN DOHERTY

RUTLEDGE HILL PRESS

NASHVILLE

Other Books of Mort Künstler's Works

Mort Künstler's 50 Epic Paintings of America
Images of the Civil War—The Paintings of Mort Künstler
Gettysburg—The Paintings of Mort Künstler

Published in Nashville, Tennessee, by Rutledge Hill Press, Inc., 211 Seventh Avenue North, Nashville, Tennessee 37219. Distributed in Canada by H. B. Fenn & Company, Ltd., 1090 Lorimar Drive, Mississauga, Ontario L5S 1R7.

Illustrations on pages 24 and 25 copyright © 1966 National Geographic Society.
Illustrations on pages 40, 43, 47, 84, 158, 160, and 218 copyright © 1976, 1977 Fleetwood, Division of Unicover Corporation, Cheyenne, Wyoming.
Illustrations on pages 60, 89, 151, 172, 216, and 217 copyright © 1984, 1985, 1986 Fleetwood, Division of Unicover Corporation, Cheyenne, Wyoming.
Epilogue copyright © 1994 Rodney O. Gragg

Designers: Peter Bradford and Anne Todd

Printed and bound in Hong Kong through Palace Press.

Library of Congress Cataloging-in-Publication Data

Künstler, Mort.
    The American spirit : the paintings of Mort Künstler / text by Henry Steele Commager and Rod Gragg ; biography by M. Stephen Doherty ; foreword by Armand Hammer.—Rev. ed.
        p.   cm.
    Includes index.
    ISBN 1-55853-309-5
    1. Künstler, Mort—Catalogs.   2. United States in art—Catalogs.   I. Commager, Henry Steele, 1902–
II. Gragg, Rod.   III. Title.
ND237.K76A4   1994
759.13—dc20   94-29044
                                                  CIP

1 2 3 4 5 6 7 8 9—99 98 97 96 95 94

Pages 1 and 2:
WILD HORSE MESA (Detail).

ACKNOWLEDGMENTS

A book of this type takes literally hundreds of people to make it possible. Although the names are too numerous to mention here, I sincerely thank them all for their hard work and indulgence. However, certain people deserve special thanks and appreciation.

This second edition of *The American Spirit* would never have come to be if it were not for the initial idea, encouragement, and support of Ron Pitkin and Larry Stone. They both contributed immeasurably and with great patience and expertise. My sincere appreciation to the late Dr. Armand Hammer for his interest in my work through the years and his kind words in the foreword. Henry Steele Commager has once again written a spellbinding text for this, our third collaboration. Knowing him and his wife, Mary, has truly been a privilege. My admiration to Steve Doherty for his diligence in the pursuit of facts and people from my past. My thanks to my good friend, Rod Gragg, for his magnificent essay on the American spirit.

My gratitude, once again, to Richard Lynch of Hammer Galleries for bringing my paintings to the attention of the art world.

I cannot thank my daughter, Jane, enough for her endless involvement in this book project, as well as her patience and understanding. Both she and Paula McEvoy have been invaluable in managing the everyday tasks of a busy studio, allowing me the time to paint.

And last, but certainly not least, my heartfelt thanks to my beautiful wife, Deborah, who had faith in me right from the start.

CONTENTS

ARTIST'S STATEMENT

TO DEBORAH
The best thing that ever
happened to me

The paintings that appear on these pages were done over a period of forty years. Many of them, certainly most of those executed before 1977, were done as illustrations commissioned by publishers and advertising agencies. Those paintings were reproduced in magazines, posters, and books. In 1977, I had my first public showing of original paintings, and from that time on, I began painting pictures with the intention that the originals would be viewed and judged on their own merit, not as an accompaniment to text. I believe the quality has improved since then, not because of the change in how they would be seen or whether they were commissioned, but simply because with practice, hard work, and greater experience, I have grown better. I hope the paintings I do ten years from now will be better still.

It has been claimed that my paintings have great accuracy. Obviously, now that I have the means to do extensive research, visit sites, and consult with authorities, my recent work is generally more precise. However, I do see errors occasionally and wish I could call many pieces back to make the necessary corrections. Of course, this is impossible. But the intent, the striving for accuracy has always been there.

This book is a collection of my best paintings, and also a book on American history because, without realizing it at the time, I have painted much of our history through the years. None of the paintings that appear here were done specifically for this book. Therefore, many great and important historical events are overlooked, and many inconsequential and fictional events are depicted.

I can only hope that the reader enjoys these paintings as much as I have enjoyed creating them!

FOREWORD   By Dr. Armand Hammer

I was privileged to meet Mort Künstler in 1977, the year in which the first public exhibition of his paintings was held at the Hammer Galleries. This exhibition helped to establish Künstler as a major artist, one whose works have wide recognition and are increasingly in demand. During these past nine years, his paintings have continually confirmed his talent, and the caliber of Künstler's overall artistic output has now placed him at the forefront of contemporary realism.

Künstler's concentration on subjects relating to the American West continues a tradition stretching back to George Catlin, the early painter of American Indians, and continuing with Frederic Remington, Charles M. Russell, and Henry Farny. His range of subjects, however, extends beyond the West to include many other epochal periods of American history.

Whatever the theme, whether it is an Indian hunting party, a Civil War battle, or the launching of the space shuttle, Künstler's paintings reflect absolute historical accuracy. To achieve this, he will often spend weeks personally conducting in-depth research, interviewing one or more experts in the field he is depicting, and making dozens of on-the-spot sketches. From the arrangement of feathers in an Indian headdress to the position of bolts in an early piece of farm machinery, Künstler is not satisfied until his painting is historically and technically perfect. It is his reputation for painstaking attention to detail as well as his innate aesthetic sense that has earned him many important commissions, most recently the recording of the historic launch of the space shuttle *Columbia.*

This book offers a collection of over thirty years of Mort Künstler's paintings, all of which recreate episodes from our nation's history. These epic paintings provide a pictorial chronicle of the drama and excitement of many phases of American history so that there is appeal for both the lover of art and the student of history.

7

INTRODUCTION   By Henry Steele Commager

No other nation can boast so comprehensive a pictorial record as the American, just as no other can display so complete a literary or historical record: the explanation lies not so much in the assiduity or devotion of American artists and historians as in the simple fact that the whole of our history falls within the era of the printing press and engraving. Much of both the pictorial and the historical record began before discovery or exploration, for America was, in a sense, invented before it was discovered and imagined before it was explored. From the beginning imagination has anticipated reality and often called it into existence: thus the Indian, for example, was a creature of the imagination as well as of reality (the very name is testimony to that). In literature and in art the two were fused until they became indistinguishable.

Nor did any other nation or any other continent present a comparable challenge to art or imagination. America was from the beginning a *Novus Ordo Saeclorum* (you will find that inscription on your dollar bills), and it took the Old World two centuries to adjust to that elementary fact. It is almost impossible for us now to recover that sense of wonder and incredulity which America inspired: surely, no other event in all history so stirred or excited the popular imagination. Where had America been all these centuries; why had God hidden it from Mankind? Whence came its people, strange of color and of tongue and of faith—or, stranger still, without faith? Were they indeed men or were they monsters, the Patagonian giants, nine feet tall, who could sweep seven Spaniards to the ground with a swing of their mighty arms; the hermaphrodites of the jungles; the Pygmies who inhabited the frozen North; the men who were covered with feathers, or with one eye in the center of their foreheads, or with heads on their chests; the Amazons who used men only for breeding and then killed them? There were paintings and engravings to prove all of this! Nature was no less prodigious and no less incomprehensible: the mountains that soared fifty thousand feet into the skies, the vast swamps and marshes with their noxious fumes, the swarms of venomous insects that darkened the skies, the poisonous snakes that swung from tree to tree, the frogs that bellowed like bulls. How to explain a world unlike any other that had ever been known?

Page 8:
ON TO RICHMOND (Detail)

9

How but by a pictorial record for all to see and wonder at!

In time these images faded out, but others took their place—the image of the Savage, ferocious and implacable; the image of the Savage, noble because descended from the Greeks and the Trojans, or from the Lost Tribes of Israel, or from Madoc, King of the Welsh, or noble because Nature had endowed him with nobility, as it had endowed the Vikings and the Tahitians and other primitive peoples. Along with all these romantic pictures of the Indian went even more romantic elaborations on the symbols of the New World. Thus Jan Mostaert's almost Gothic recreation of an imaginary West Indian Scene, complete with naked figures who might have come out of the Garden of Eden, or Tiepolo's gorgeous symbol of a voluptuous American astride an alligator, in the Residenz in Wurzburg, or his equally romantic fresco of the New World paying homage to Spain, on the ceiling of the Royal Palace in Madrid. This kind of symbolic painting persisted well into the nineteenth century in the exotic and sinister jungle scenes of Mexico and Brazil created by Henri Rousseau.

Thus, from the beginning and down to our own day the spectacle of Nature in America fired the artistic imagination. The English-born Thomas Cole, who painted not only *The Course of Empire,* but as William Cullen Bryant remarked, "scenes of wild grandeur peculiar to our own country," observed accurately enough that "the painter of American scenery has privileges superior to any other . . . for all Nature here is new to art."

The record of what is now America begins in the mid-sixteenth century with Jacques Le Moyne's paintings of the Indians and Nature in Florida—known to us only through copies by John White, who had already painted the Eskimos of Baffin Bay. A few years later, White recreated life on Roanoke Island, where Raleigh had planted his "lost" colony. Le Moyne, who pictured the French commander Laudonnière conferring with the Indian chief Athore, anticipated John Bartram's painting of an alligator fight in the Florida swamps; moreover, he catered to European notions of American savagery with his pictures of the dismembering of captives and of cannibalism. White, in contrast, painted some seventy watercolors which celebrated rather the domestic than the savage side of Indian life. Soon that master editor and entrepreneur, Teodor De Bry, was engraving everything Le Moyne and White had provided, and much more, too—he illustrated Hakluyt's *Voyages* and John Smith's *General History* and engraved Albert Eckout's dramatic paintings of the flora and fauna of Brazil. For two centuries Europe's vision of America was to be that which De Bry had conjured up. It was even to some degree the new world vision as well; for Father Lafitau in his fascinating volume on *The Customs of the American Indians Compared with the Customs of Primitive Tribes* took De Bry's Indians and made them into Greek and Trojan warriors!

From these earliest beginnings, the illustration of America was to be a ceaseless occupation and preoccupation of artists from both Old World and New. The obsession with Indians was, if anything, more pronounced among European than among American artists. Thus we have a whole gallery of Indian paintings by Francisco Goya, Eugéne Delacroix, Karl Bodmer, Jean Millet, and Rosa Bonheur—and from the anglicized American, Benjamin West, whose fascination with the Indians appears in his *Death of Wolfe*, as in his earlier painting of *Penn's Treaty with the Indians*. But it was George Catlin of Pennsylvania who dedicated his artistic life to the singleminded study of the Indian, for, as he wrote, "the history and customs of such a people, preserved by pictorial illustration, are themes worthy of the lifetime of one man, and nothing short of the loss of my life shall prevent me from becoming their historian." Their historian he did indeed become. His more than six hundred paintings of the American Indian is the most comprehensive as it is the most realistic celebration of the life and character of the native races that has yet been made, and has inspired a long line of illustrious successors such as Frederic Remington, Charles Russell, Henry Farny, and, in our own day, Mort Künstler.

From the beginning, too, Europeans were fascinated by the limitless variety and abundance of the flora and fauna of the New World. As early as the 1720s the English-born Mark Catesby came to the New World to study and paint its plants, animals, and birds. His *Natural History of Carolina, Florida and the Bahama Islands*, published in London and on the continent in two sumptuous volumes, presented some three hundred specimens—all engraved and colored by Catesby himself—to an astonished and delighted Europe. Two of Catesby's greatest successors were also foreign-born, though both developed their interests and their skills in America: Alexander Wilson of Scotland and John James Audubon, born of French parents in Santo Domingo. Harried out of Scotland as a dangerous radical, Wilson found refuge in Pennsylvania, where he early came under the influence of the great botanist William Bartram. Bartram, who had also described and illustrated the flora and fauna of

Florida and the Carolinas, inspired Wilson to the study of American nature. Without other artistic or scientific training, Wilson set himself the herculean task of recording and illustrating each American bird: by prodigious industry he succeeded in depicting over 260 in eight magnificent folio volumes during the last seven years of his tragically short life. His contemporary, Audubon, ranged more widely. His *Birds of America*—with elaborate text—displayed some five hundred species in more than a thousand colored engravings. Later in life he undertook a similar illustrated survey of the *Quadrupeds of America,* an enterprise which his son brought to completion.

Thus, the artistic discovery of the United States was launched at the very beginning of the history of the republic and proved a continuous process for another century. All through the nineteenth century veritable armies of naturalists, explorers, ethnologists, surveyors, map-makers, geologists, botanists, and what we would now call cultural anthropologists spread out across the country, drawing or painting—later photographing—every feature of nature and life in the vast American continent. Artists accompanied the geological and railroad surveys and military expeditions (including naval); they went with the covered wagons that crossed the Plains and the mountains, they sailed on flatboats and steamboats along rivers, canals, and lakes. They were fascinated by the railroad trains that crossed the Alleghenies and reached out to the Mississippi and the Great Plains, and delighted by the contrast of Indians and buffalo racing the new steam monsters. One and all they might have said, with Robert Louis Stevenson, "what was Troytown to this!" The demand for their work was insatiable. Every Victorian parlor table held a copy of *Picturesque America* or *The National Portrait Gallery,* with their hundreds of illustrations of the American scene and of American statesmen and soldiers and men of letters. Soon the firm of Currier and Ives was printing millions of lithographs, sentimental, romantic, and nostalgic; soon, too, every respectable mantelpiece boasted one of John Roger's bronze or plaster figures—*Checkers on the Farm, Lincoln Emancipating the Slaves,* or *Rip Van Winkle*—"illustrations" depicting an American past as piously as those of Currier and Ives.

More important was the emergence of a host of illustrated magazines designed for every audience: from lurid scenes of city life in the *Police Gazette* to the fashionable women of *Godey's Ladies Book;* from *Harper's Weekly,* which employed Winslow Homer to sketch scenes from the Civil War (he called himself "just a reporter") and Thomas Nast to excoriate Tammany Hall and the Tweed Ring, to *Frank Leslie's Illustrated Weekly*, which employed scores of engravers to cover the whole social, military, and political scene. Best of all were the new monthly magazines that specialized in artistic illustrations: *Scribner's, Harper's,* and *The Century*, which produced the lavishly illustrated *Battles and Leaders of the Civil War,* and the ever-beloved *St. Nicholas Magazine.* Soon every artist was painting for "St. Nick" (as every writer was writing for it)—Arthur Rackham and Maxfield Parrish and Howard Pyle, who founded a school; N. C. Wyeth and E. W. Kemble, best remembered for his drawings of Uncle Remus; Palmer Cox, who invented the Brownies; the delicate Reginald Birch; and scores of others who made *St. Nicholas* the most lavishly and beautifully illustrated of all general magazines. We have nothing like it now.

From Thucydides to Winston Churchill, history has been recorded in massive volumes; from the artists responsible for Pompeii's frescos to Goya and Delacroix, and, in our own country, from Benjamin West to Winslow Homer and Thomas Hart Benton, it has been recorded just as fully in art and mostly in the art of illustration. The sheer volume is overwhelming: George Groce and David Wallace list some 12,000 American artists and designers before the year 1860; the number since then must be countless. We could begin with Benjamin West or Paul Revere's engraving of the Boston Massacre or Amos Doolittle's engravings of the battles of Lexington and Concord. Better yet, we could begin with that impressive galaxy of painters and illustrators who recorded the struggle for independence and limned the great heroes of that struggle: with John Trumbull and Charles Willson Peale and Gilbert Stuart, who painted scores of Washingtons. Between them they recorded every chapter and every episode of the birth of the nation. We take this for granted, but what would we not give now for an authentic portrayal of Remus and Romulus and the founding of Rome, of Hengist and Horsa landing on the shores of Britain in 449, of King Arthur at his Round Table, of Roland sounding his mighty horn at Roncesvalles, of Dannebrog floating down from Heaven at the battle of Lindanaes that June day, 1219—a sure sign of divine favor for Valdemar the Victorious.

Every chapter, nay every page, of our own history has been elaborately recorded in engraving or painting—the victory at Yorktown, and Benjamin West's unfinished, but impressive, painting of Jay, Adams, Franklin, and Laurens signing the Treaty of Peace with Britain. We could go on and on, to the storming of the beaches of Normandy and the landing on the moon—which Mort Künstler gives us in this volume.

In all this the line between "art" and "illustration," never very clear, evaporates. It is commonly asserted that illustration differs from art because it is inexorably tied to the subject matter—to the event, to the written page, to facts. True enough, but so is a portrait by a Whistler, an Eakins, a Sargent. So, too, needless to say, is the vast archive of historical painting. We do not label West or Turner, Goya or Delacroix, "illustrators" because they provided us with authentic recreations of great moments in history.

Trumbull's *Declaration of Independence*, Vanderlyn's *Landing of Columbus*, George Bingham's *Fur Traders*, Morse's *Lafayette*, Durand's *Kindred Spirits*, Healy's dramatic recreation of Webster delivering his address on "Liberty and Union," Carpenter's *Signing of the Emancipation Proclamation*, Eakins's *Gross Clinic*, Grant Wood's *American Gothic*, and Mort Künstler's portrait of *Sharp Eyes* do not cease to be art because they are authentic historical illustrations.

The best of these illustrations were not merely photographic reproductions; some artists were forced, of necessity, to fall back on an imaginative recreation of the past—how else present Columbus's landfall on Hispañola or the surrender of Cornwallis at Yorktown. But for the best of them, Frank Weitenkampf's conclusion is valid: illustrations "are not only the picturing of society's outward manifestations, but the implication of its deeper impulses, ideals, and strivings." Clearly that judgment is valid for our greatest illustrators—for those who recorded the stirring events of the past, for those who preserved for us the life of the Indians, for those who went across the mountains and over the plains and on the trails to Oregon and California, for those who plunged into the tragedies and heroisms of the Civil War, for those who caught the realities of industrialism and farming and labor, for those who limned society in all its varied and highly nationalistic manifestations, for those who recognized that the steamboat and the railroad train and the airplane were no less romantic than the covered wagon, for those who responded to the excitement of the greatest of experiments in democracy and gave us democracy in action. Clearly it is true for Mort Künstler's illustrations of the whole range of American experience from the emergence of an Indian civilization to the launching of the space shuttle.

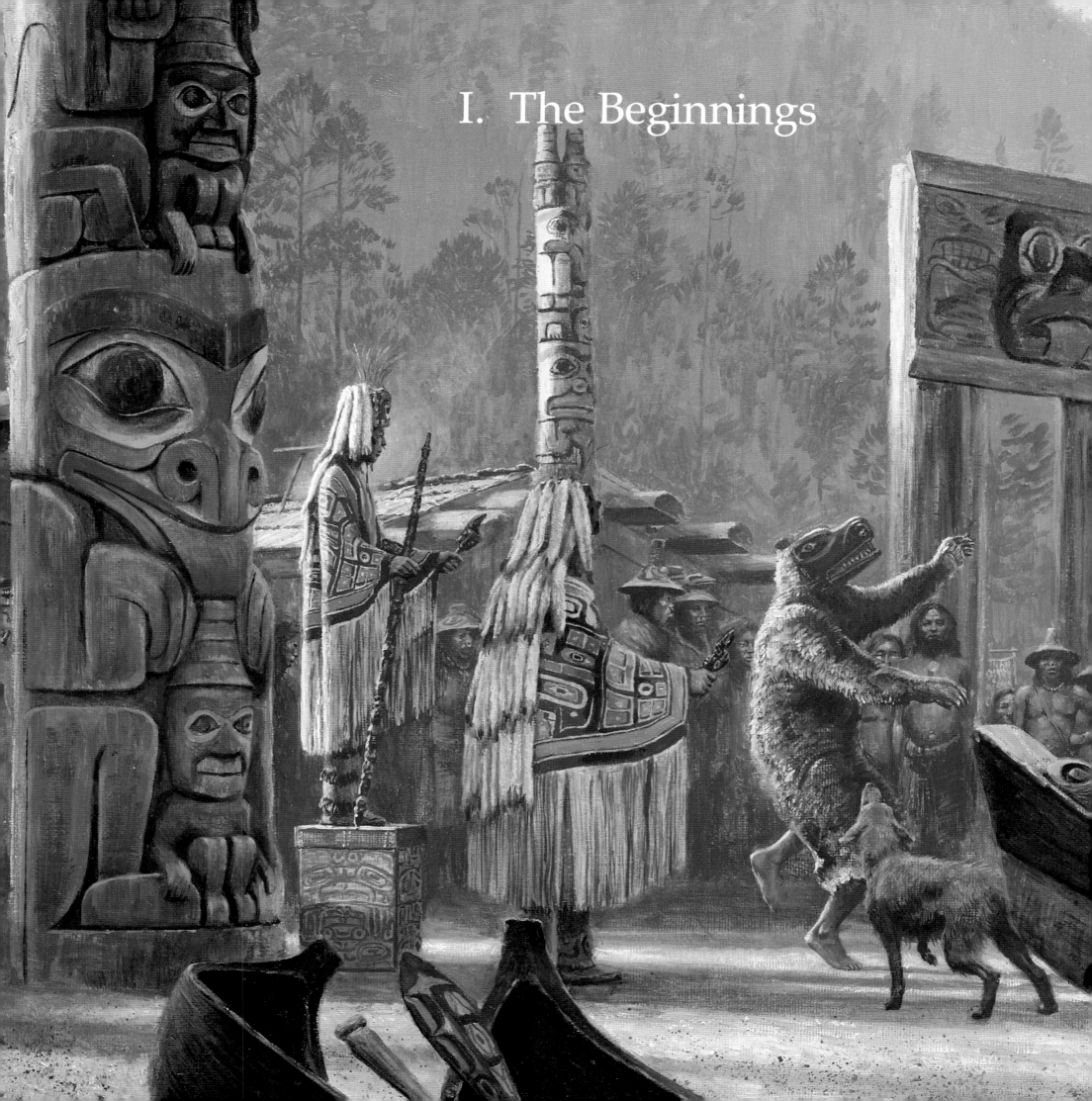

I. The Beginnings

I: THE BEGINNINGS

The white man is a comparative newcomer to the American continents. Those whom Columbus called "Indians," because he fondly imagined that he had reached India, were the first and, for thirty or forty thousand years, the only inhabitants of America. Sometime in that dim prehistoric past, Mongolian huntsmen and their families, fleeing, perhaps, from more warlike enemies, crossed from the easternmost promontory of Siberia to the Big and Little Diomede Islands and then to Seward Peninsula, the westernmost point of the American continent. In the following millennia there were innumerable other crossings. Gradually, these Mongolian peoples spread out over the whole of the Americas: by the time of the European "discovery" there were perhaps thirty or more million "Indians" differing in language, culture, civilization, even in appearance, quite as markedly as did the peoples of the African, Asian, or European continents. Mr. Künstler has given us here an imaginative, authentic reconstruction of a familiar, mayhap a daily scene, among the ancestors of the Paiutes who settled in the desert country of the Southwest.

Page 15:
HAIDA BEAR DANCE
(Detail)

Left:
ANCESTORS OF THE PAIUTE: THE DESERT CULTURE, 3000 B.C. 1976.
Oil on canvas, 28x40 in.
Collection Favell Museum, Klamath Falls, Oregon.
"This picture shows the return of a successful hunting party to their cave shelter. The man in the foreground is making duck decoys out of tule, while the man behind him repairs a net used to catch small game. The Paiutes were such excellent weavers that their woven jugs were virtually watertight."

Right:
HAIDA BEAR DANCE. 1987.
Oil on canvas, 36x52 in.
Collection of the artist.
"This depicts the arrival of the Eagle Clan at the village of the Raven Clan for a potlatch. *Potlatch*, **which means 'give away' in Chinook, was a custom practiced by almost every Northwest Coast Indian tribe."**

More than any other part of America, the Northwest coast—from Alaska to Puget Sound—was to be the crossroads of civilizations. The Haida, and other Northwest coastal tribes, had developed an advanced and complex civilization long before the coming of the Europeans. In the seventeenth and eighteenth centuries, the Spanish, the Russians, and the British contested for control of the coast all the way down to the Bay of Saint Francis; in the 1790s the newly independent Americans discovered its wealth of fur and its potentialities for the China trade, and joined in the struggle. In that process the highly developed Indian culture was subverted and largely destroyed.

A picturesque and dramatic part of the Northwest Indian's social life was the "potlatch" ceremony, practiced throughout the area. Its accompanying richly carved totem poles, splendidly decorated canoes, and ostentatious insignia and costumes of office and rank were as elaborate as any at the fabled Court of King Arthur. The potlatch ceremony, which combined the giving of lavish gifts with the destruction of property—the latter occurring well after contact with white civilization—has something of the social and psychological significance found in the ceremonial extravagances of the very rich in capitalist civilizations.

HAIDA WELCOME. 1983.
Oil on board, 19x22 in.
Collection Adam Z. Saks.

Right:
HAIDA HEADMAN. 1983.
Oil on board, 15⅝x19⅝ in.
Collection Mr. H. Lee Turner.
"I have become quite expert on the Haida. My research has taken me to the Museum of the American Indian, the American Museum of Natural History, and sites in British Columbia, and I have consulted with Dr. Philip Drucker of the University of Kentucky and Dr. George Dalton of Northwestern University. I find the Northwest coastal tribes quite interesting, and intend to continue painting them in the future."

THE MAYFLOWER COMPACT. 1985. Opaque watercolor, 12x15¼ in. Collection Hammer Galleries, New York.

Not in ancient Greece, nor in the Magna Carta, but in the signing of the Mayflower Compact, pictured above, is the true beginning of democracy in America. Here for the first time in history all men came together and made a government. Here, too, was the remote antecedent of the Declaration of Independence, which asserted that "governments are instituted among men, deriving their just powers from the consent of the governed." Thus during the brief seventy years of its history the Plymouth Colony bequeathed to all future generations a special heritage and a special romance.

America's first great westward expansion began in 1540, when Hernando de Soto moved west from Florida. He encountered what were, in all likelihood, the most civilized of the eastern tribes: the Creeks, Cherokees, Choctaw, Natchez, and Seminole. These Indians had developed tribal domains throughout the Ohio Valley and into Florida; they had stable agricultural economies, and rude, but effective, forms of government. They had independent languages; one nation, the Cherokee, had a written alphabet that later enabled them to translate the Bible. No wonder that these Indians were labeled the Five Civilized Tribes by the Americans who followed them into—who pushed them from—their ancestral lands.

With the other cultural developments came a body of social and religious festivals and practices. One of the most interesting of these was the Green Corn Ceremony—a combination of New Year's and Thanksgiving Day—practiced not only by the Creek, pictured here, but by all the southeastern tribes. Designed to celebrate the ripening of that corn which was the basic food for the region and marking also the passing of the old year, the ceremony was attended by elaborate dances and feasts; by fasting, celibacy, and other forms of self-denial; by amnesty and forgiveness (even of debts); by a general refurbishing of the village—both the houses and the public buildings. It would be difficult to find a more complex, more complete, celebration of both atonement and redemption in any modern religion.

The fate of the Creeks was a tragic one. Some of them followed the great Tecumseh (defeated by the Americans at the Battle of Tippecanoe) and later the British in the War of 1812. For this, in part, they incurred the enmity of white settlers: their greater "crime" was title to some of the best lands in the region. Thus, they, with other members of the Five Civilized Tribes guilty of similar "crimes," were removed to the new Oklahoma Territory. It is not clear whether the Green Corn Ceremony was maintained in the Indian Territory, as it came to be called, but if it was, the emphasis should have been on retribution rather than regeneration. For that "removal" was one of the most tragic—and most disgraceful—chapters in the annals of American history.

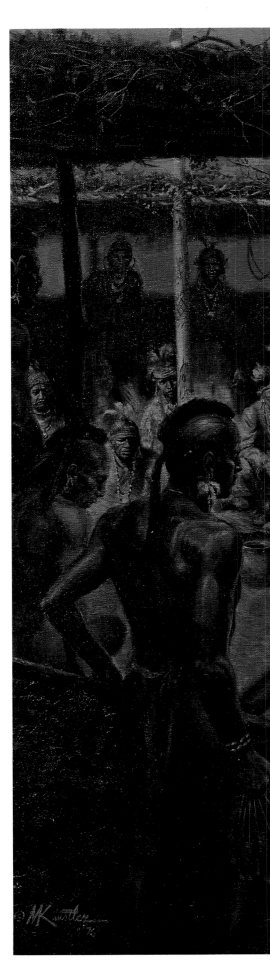

GREEN CORN CEREMONY OF THE CREEK. 1976. Oil on canvas, 28x40 in. Collection Mr. Harry Glass.

Left:
MIDÉWIWIN CEREMONY OF THE OJIBWAY CHIPPEWA. 1977. Oil on canvas, 28x40 in. Collection Mr. Harry Glass.
"The ceremonial lodge is portrayed during the initiation of a new member into the Midéwiwin, an exclusive society of shamans, or medicine men. The four grades of the society are indicated by the four posts in the rear of the ceremonial lodge. Members showed their rank by the designs and colors painted on their faces."

Right:
LOS CONQUISTADORES. 1981. Oil on board, 16x20 in. Collection Mr. Robert Anderson.

At the beginning it was Spain that created the largest of American empires, perhaps the largest of world empires: her *conquistadores* and priests overran the islands of the Caribbean, toppled the Aztec Empire in Mexico and that of the Inca in Peru, and even, for awhile, absorbed Portuguese Brazil. When the Americans made their bid for independence, the Spanish dominions in America stretched from Florida westward to the Pacific, from the Straits of Magellan all the way north to the Bay of Saint Francis and even to Nootka Bay on Vancouver Island. That empire endured in one way or another for four centuries—from the first landfall of Columbus in 1492 to the Cuban War of 1898, which finally ousted Spain from her last American stronghold. Yet, although the Spanish empire is gone, Spanish culture and language and faith linger on: even today the Iberian languages are spoken by more people in the two American continents than English.

It was Ponce de Leon, seeking the Fountain of Youth, who first explored Florida—and named it; De Soto traversed it and claimed it for Spain, but after his departure, the French established a Huguenot settlement on Saint John's River. Spain reacted by capturing the French fort and either killing or dispersing the settlers. Thereafter, Spanish hegemony in the Floridas—West and East alike—was not seriously challenged for a century nor ended for more than two. Francis Drake had burned the first permanent Spanish settlement at Saint Augustine in 1586, but the English triumph was fleeting, as fleeting as the French had been.

Here, in meticulous detail, we have the building, in the early 1670s, of the fortress of Castillo de San Marcos at Saint Augustine; its outer walls fourteen feet thick at the base and nine at the top, the fort was built with such resilience from seashells cemented by their own lime and held together by oyster shells that, as a frustrated English attacker complained, "the rock will not splinter but will give way to a cannon ball as though you would stick a knife into cheese." The rock did not give away, despite repeated assaults by Spain's enemies.

Left:
THE BUILDING OF CASTILLO DE SAN MARCOS, SAINT AUGUSTINE, FLORIDA. 1965. Oil on illustration board, 25x32½ in. Collection National Geographic Society. "For these paintings on pages 24 and 25 I went directly to Saint Augustine, where I was helped in my research by consultations with historians from the National Park Service. My knowledge of Spanish came in handy, as I found myself poring through old archives at the fort—a part of the job I found particularly fascinating."

Right:
BATTLE FOR SAINT AUGUSTINE, 1703—AGONY OF A TOWN AFLAME. 1965. Oil on illustration board, 22x34 in. Collection National Geographic Society.

Right:
BIG HEAD DANCER. 1977.
Oil on canvas, 20x16 in.
Collection Lowie Museum of
Anthropology, Berkeley,
California.

Left:
KUKSU CEREMONY OF
THE POMO. 1977. Oil on
canvas, 28x40 in. Collection
Favell Museum, Klamath
Falls, Oregon.
"I was aided in my research
on this California tribe by
Fritz Riddell, an historian/
anthropologist with the
California Department of
Parks. He arranged for
Marvin Lee, a Maidu Indian,
to pose in costumes supplied
by the Lowie Museum of
Anthropology in Berkeley."

The Kuksu ceremony of the Pomo—one of the many small but (compared to other Indians in more desolate regions) "rich" tribes of northern California—depicted here is not dissimilar from the Green Corn Ceremony of the southeastern nations. It too was designed to celebrate a benign harvest, perhaps a new year. However, unlike the Green Corn Ceremony, which was generally celebrated by the entire tribe, the festival was dominated by members of the Kuksu Cult. A secret society widespread throughout the northern California tribes, the Kuksu Cult called for its members to impersonate supernatural beings associated with the origin of the world. It required elaborate masks and disguises, ceremonial robes and ornaments. The celebration, which lasted for four days, was not unlike the Kachina dances practiced by the Indians of the Southwest; yet, although it may be romantic to think of Pueblo Indians migrating westward, the evidence is not conclusive.

The Pomo Indians lived in relative isolation until the discovery of gold in California in 1848. The subsequent "rush" into the territory by the "forty-niners"—gold-seekers little interested in the preservation of native cultures and ceremonies—marked the beginning of the disintegration of the northern California tribes. While still noted for their excellent basketry, the Pomo have largely assimilated into the white population.

As the United States was the first nation in history to be "brought forth," it lacked many of what had long been assumed were essential attributes of nationalism: history, legends, traditions, national institutions, songs, ballads, and heroes. Somehow it supplied itself with these in record time. Perhaps it was the heroes who came first, and what a remarkable galaxy they were: Franklin, Washington, Jefferson, Adams, Madison, Noah Webster. But it was not only those Jefferson called "demigods" who were essential to nationalism; equally important—especially in a country made by the people themselves—were popular heroes. These too, thanks to a classless society, thanks to opportunity and the habits of individual initiative, soon emerged.

No one was more essentially "popular" than Daniel Boone, who was popular in the sense that he was almost a contrived hero, a symbol of the pioneer, the Indian fighter, the trailblazer. Boone was by no means the "first" person to "discover" the Kentucky country, or to blaze a way through the Cumberland Gap to the richest empire in the world. But he was the one who caught the popular imagination, not only in America but even in the Old World. Thus, over in England, Lord Byron, seeking a foil to the corrupt "heroes" of the Old World in his epic *Don Juan*, celebrated the heroism of Boone:

> *Of the great names which in our faces stare,*
> *The General Boone, back-woodsman of Kentucky,*
> *Was happiest amongst mortals anywhere....*

DANIEL BOONE, 1984.
Opaque watercolor, 15x13½
in. Collection Hammer
Galleries, New York.

Born in Pennsylvania in 1734, Boone lived a long and adventurous life on a succession of frontiers. A hunter at the age of twelve, he served in Braddock's ill-fated campaign of 1755, and a decade later made his first foray into Kentucky. After a protracted journey to that enchanting land he became an agent of Richard Henderson of North Carolina, who was planting a colony in what was then called Transylvania. It was in that capacity that Boone marked out the "Wilderness Road" and established a series of small settlements, one of them appropriately named Boonesboro.

Captured by the fierce Shawnees in 1778, he was not slaughtered but adopted by them. Aware that Boonesboro was to be attacked, he managed to escape in time to warn the settlement and to defend it against attackers. This, more than any other action, made him a folk hero.

THE FIRST TANNER IN
AMERICA. 1972. Oil on
board, 28x38 in. Collection
American Cyanamid
Company.

Pages 30-31:
FOX HOLLOW FARM.
1984. Oil on canvas, 24x48
in. Collection Mr. Jack
Morse.
"Commissioned by Jack
Morse, the present owner of
Fox Hollow Farm on Long
Island, this painting shows
how the farm might have
looked in 1750. I used the
Morse family as models for
the painting; my dog Candy
is on the right."

The discovery of America opened a new era in human
history. Every nation of the Old World rushed in to seize
land, exploit natural resources—chiefly precious metals—and,
as a kind of afterthought, Christianize the native peoples.
Spain and Portugal led the way, staking out almost limitless
claims throughout South America and in much of North
America. The Russians, sweeping irresistibly across Siberia,
took over Alaska and built outposts down the Pacific coast
almost to San Francisco Bay. France followed, its intrepid
explorers and missionaries taking over what is now Canada,
the "Old Northwest" along the Great Lakes, and laying
claim to a vast territory reaching west to the Rocky Mountains. Holland and Sweden both planted tiny colonies on
the Atlantic coast, but these did not survive. It was England, last in the field, that proved the most successful in
North America. Alone among the European powers she
colonized the Atlantic coast from what is now Maine to
Georgia, transplanting English institutions of government
and law, and habits of freedom and independence.

The new economic-political system called mercantilism—a kind of early "military-commercial-industrial complex"—dictated a struggle between the European powers for
control of the continent (a continent that, in the words of

ROGER'S RANGERS. 1982. Oil on canvas, 25x34 in. Collection Lucy and John H. Epstein.
"The exploits of Major Robert Rogers, as related in the great novel *Northwest Passage* by Kenneth Rogers, were the inspiration for this painting of Rogers and his men behind enemy lines during his famous raid on Saint Francis in the French and Indian War."

Pages 34-35:
DISCOVERY BY MISTAKE – PORTOLA DISCOVERS SAN FRANCISCO BAY. 1970. Oil on board, 24x48 in. Collection San Mateo County Historical Museum, San Mateo, California.
"The museum commissioned me to do this painting after seeing one I had painted on the same subject for National Geographic. After visiting the site (there are poplars on the hillside now, and down by the bay where the marshes once were is now the San Francisco airport) I went on to Tucson to consult with authorities on the expedition. The *soldados de cuera* with their leather jackets, shields, and horse armor are rarely seen in paintings."

Thomas Jefferson, had "room for our descendants to the thousandth and thousandth generation"). The result of this competition was an interminable series of wars, fought from Newfoundland to the Caribbean, from the Atlantic to the Mississippi and beyond, and in the frozen reaches of Hudson's Bay and Alaska.

That two centuries of conflict came to a climax in the mid-eighteenth century in what Europeans called the Seven Years War and Americans the French and Indian War. It was waged by the soldiers of France and England, by hastily recruited colonials and French Canadians, by a score of Indian tribes, and by backwoodsmen and Indian fighters like Robert Rogers and his Rangers, who seemed to show up wherever the fighting was hottest—and the rewards most lucrative! Rogers's untrained, almost savage followers fought with Governor Johnson at Fort Niagara, with General Amherst at Crown Point and Ticonderoga, and at distant Michilimakinac at the junction of Lake Huron and Lake Michigan—a thousand miles to the west—and in the final battle of the war, the capture of Montreal in 1760, and then, even after France had succumbed, against Chief Pontiac and his Indian "rebels."

That victory meant that the English-speaking peoples could long dominate most of North America; it meant, too, the beginning of the end of Old World dominion over the New. All that took another century or more—a century that saw the independence of the United States and of the states of Latin America, the elimination of Russia from Alaska, and, with the Spanish American War, the final disappearance of Spain from the New World.

Baja (or Lower) California was originally believed to be an island, but by the mid-sixteenth century was recognized as a peninsula attached to the mainland of North America. Spanish sailors had traveled along the coast as far north as Monterey Bay. For the next two centuries, sailors continued to chart the coast, searching for the fabled Straits of Anian and safe harbors for the very real Manilla Galleons. Such expeditions caused priests—dreaming of the innumerable "lost souls" to be discovered and converted to Christianity—to call for further explorations; the Spanish Crown, engaged in almost incessant warfare in the Old World and disappointed by bleak reports (such as that of Coronado who

in the 1540s had ranged as far from Mexico as Kansas) of never-ending deserts and grasslands, countless herds of buffalo, and tribes of hostile Indians (but never any gold) in the New World north of the Rio Grande, wanted no part of further expansion, which could only drain the already depleted national treasury.

In the Caribbean, Florida, and the Argentine, the imperial designs of other nations had forced Spain to send out colonizers to unsettled regions to hold Spanish claims. Likewise, Russian movement down from Alaska in the mid-eighteenth century renewed royal interest in California. Moving out from the established settlements in Baja, Spanish sailors, soldiers, and priests traveled by land and sea, choosing sites for the string of mission-forts that were to dominate the area for nearly a century. Beginning with San Diego, settled in 1769, the Spaniards moved northward until they occupied San Francisco in 1776.

Never successful at attracting many colonists to her California possessions, Spain was fortunate in holding the area for so long. The Mexicans, winning California along with their independence in 1821, were not so lucky. The very bay that excited the members of the Portolá expedition also excited the expanding American Republic in search of a port for the China trade. How ironic that California, lost to the Spanish speaking peoples in 1848, would prove to be the long-sought, but always elusive, *El Dorado*—the land of gold.

II. The New Nation

II. THE NEW NATION

The beginnings of America are lost in the dim past of pre-history; the beginnings of the American Republic can be dated, with some accuracy, from the Declaration of Independence, which for the first time in all history called a new nation into being. The Declaration, written by Jefferson, passed by the Continental Congress on July 2 and signed by most of its members on July 4, 1776, set forth with incomparable eloquence not only the causes that impelled the American people to declare their independence but the philosophy that inspired that declaration and was to animate the new nation.

When the Declaration was proclaimed, the war for independence was already well under way: Washington had triumphed at Boston, now he was facing disaster in New York. On the very day the Congress had voted independence, General Howe landed 10,000 redcoats on Staten Island: a few days later his brother, Admiral Howe, sailed in with 150 transports, crowded with troops and supplies. It was at this dark hour that a copy of the Declaration reached Washington. He promptly ordered "that the several brigades are to be drawn up this evening on their respective Parades, at six o'clock, when the Declaration of Congress . . . is to be read in an audible voice." At that hour soldiers and officers took their place on the parade-ground —what is now, in all likelihood, City Hall Park in lower Manhattan—and the commander of each brigade read out the historic phrases: *"When, in the course of human events. . . . WE hold these truths to be self-evident. . . ."*

The origin of the American flag is not quite as spectacular as that of the Danish flag, Dannebrog, which fell from Heaven at the battle of Lindanaes in 1219, but it may be as legendary. It was, surprisingly enough, not until June 14, 1777, that Congress adopted an American flag of "thirteen stripes, alternate red and white; that the union be thirteen stars, white, in a blue field representing a new constellation." The tradition that Washington himself asked Betsy Ross, a war-widow who kept an upholsterer's shop in Philadelphia, to sew the flag, however, was first launched

Page 37:
LAFAYETTE WITH WASHINGTON AT MORRISTOWN (Detail)

Right:
READING THE DECLARATION OF INDEPENDENCE TO THE TROOPS. 1975. Oil on canvas, 28x38 in. Collection Federal Hall National Memorial, New York.

by her grandson in 1880. Yet it may be valid: after all the Pennsylvania Naval Board had paid her fourteen pounds, twelve shilling, and two pence for making "ship's colors," and it was aboardship—John Paul Jones flew the new flag on *The Ranger*—that the national banner was first used. Widely accepted, the flag knew many designs until 1818, when Congress decided on its final dimensions and form—thirteen stripes, and one star for every state in the Union.

The adoption of a national flag was part of a much larger and more significant enterprise: that of providing the new nation with the symbols, heroes, and legends traditionally associated with nationalism—and so essential to a new people without a national past. In short, a Usable Past was created. Betsy Ross was as much a necessary part of that past as Captain Parker at Lexington Common or Washington at Valley Forge or "Mad Anthony" Wayne at Stony Brook or George Rogers Clark wading the swollen Wabash or the bands playing "The World Turned Upside Down" at Yorktown; and along with these a much more credible legend than the unforgettable images supplied by Parson Weems of Washington chopping down a cherry tree, or better yet, his entering heaven.

Much of nationalism—and of patriotism—is a matter of symbols; and of these, none was more admired than those connected with heroes and battles. In all this the new United States was fortunate, for the Revolution was a veritable cornucopia of heroic episodes and memories: not only heroic visions such as Washington crossing the Delaware, but heroic words as well. What schoolchild fails to recognize the stirring call to battle of Captain John Parker at Lexington Common, "If they mean to have a war, let it start here!"; or the warning of Colonel Prescott at Bunker Hill, "Don't shoot until you see the whites of their eyes!"; or Patrick Henry's demand before the Virginia Assembly to "give me liberty or give me death!"; or the noble sentiments of Nathan Hale, ascending the gallows, "I only regret that I have but one life to lose for my country!" And the most memorable of all, the cry attributed to John Paul Jones when his ship, the *Bonhomme Richard*, closed with the *Serapis* off the coast of Scotland on September 23, 1779.

Earlier, in the spring of 1778, Jones had been active off the Scottish coast, capturing no less than seven ships and scores of prisoners. The following winter the French

THE STARS AND STRIPES ARE BORN. 1977. Oil on board, 19⅝x20¾ in. Collection Mr. Homer Noble.

king supplied him with an old ship, which Jones refitted and named in honor of Benjamin Franklin's *Poor Richard's Almanac.* In mid-August 1779, Jones renewed his harrying of the Scottish coast, picking up some seventeen prizes. On the 23rd of September he came up with a Baltic merchant ship, protected by *H.M.S. Serapis.* The *Bonhomme Richard*, a twelve-pounder, engaged the *Serapis,* an eighteen-pounder in a desperate contest. At one point, the *Serapis* successfully shot down the *Bonhomme Richard's* colors. Certain of victory, the British captain, Pearson, demanded Jones's surrender. Instead, he was met with the refusal, "I have not yet begun to fight!" And fight on Jones did. Closing with the *Serapis,* the American captain lashed the two ships together. Following a three-hour hand-to-hand contest, Captain Pearson surrendered. The *Bonhomme Richard* sank amidst flames, but the new nation's flag was raised on the deck of the *Serapis.*

LAFAYETTE WITH WASHINGTON AT MORRISTOWN. 1981. Oil on canvas, 36x48 in. Collection Crum and Forster, Morristown, New Jersey. "Commissioned by the Crum and Forster Insurance Company to do a scene of historic Morristown for their corporate headquarters, I decided to use the Ford Mansion as a backdrop for my painting. Washington used this building as his headquarters during the winter of 1779–80. It was in the spring of 1780 that he received from the Marquis de Lafayette the welcome news of the help he would receive from France."

Far right:
I HAVE JUST BEGUN TO FIGHT. 1977. Oil on canvas, 17x17⅞ in. Collection Mr. Homer Noble. "Research took me to the Naval Academy at Annapolis and the United States Navy Museum in Washington, D.C., where the late Commander Tad Damon, director of the museum, was of invaluable help."

On October 14, 1780, Washington named his most trusted lieutenant, Nathanael Greene, to command the American forces in the south. Greene wisely chose to follow the guerrilla tactics already being used in the area. He sent his ablest commander, Daniel Morgan, to harass British outposts in the west, where he inflicted disastrous defeats on the British at Cowpens (January 1781) and Guilford (March 1781). After trying in vain to corner Greene, Cornwallis himself retreated to Virginia. In August 1781, he occupied Yorktown—valuable because it provided access to the sea by means of the York River. There he awaited reenforcements from the British navy in the north.

Never in his career had Washington revealed higher qualities of military genius than in his response to this situation. His army was mostly in and around New York. Instantly he saw, and seized, the opportunity to smash Cornwallis. Combining the American and French armies at his command, he hurried them by forced marches to the Elk River in Virginia. There French transports brought them to Williamsburg. Meanwhile the French fleet, under Admiral DeGrasse, sailed up from the West Indies and inflicted damaging losses on the British in the Battle of the Capes off Yorktown. Now the combined army and naval forces closed in on Cornwallis.

Left:
THE CAPTURE OF FORT MOTTE. 1976. Oil on board, 30x40 in. Collection Charleston Museum, Charleston, South Carolina.

Right:
DIGGING THE TRENCHES AT YORKTOWN. 1976. Opaque watercolor, 14x22 in. Collection New York Bank for Savings.
"Trenches were dug at night to avoid enemy fire. The engineer is pointing out an enemy position to his commanding officer."

With the dispersion of the British fleet by DeGrasse, Cornwallis knew that his situation was desperate, his hope for reenforcements frustrated by the French navy. Besieged by the combined French and American land forces, he began negotiations for surrender on October 17. Humiliated and desperate, he refused to surrender in person, but delegated the disagreeable task to his second-in-command, General O'Hara. Washington, at the head of the American, and Rochambeau, at the head of the French contingent, were prepared to preside over the surrender; but in response to the Cornwallis gambit, Washington delegated his own second-in-command, General Lincoln, to receive O'Hara's sword.

As the British troops stacked their arms on October 19, 1781, their band played "The World Turned Upside Down." It was indeed; a handful of colonials had toppled the greatest power on the globe—so at least the event could be interpreted. That was, in a sense, the way the British interpreted it. "O God," cried Lord North when he heard the news, "it is all over, it is all over." And George III prepared to abdicate. The king was more perceptive than his first minister: he did not abdicate, but the resolution urging the king to end the war, which was carried in Commons in February 1782 may be regarded, symbolically at least, as the end of the long era of Royal rule in the realm of foreign affairs. Soon peace negotiations were underway, and almost miraculously the Americans outmaneuvered both the British and the French and emerged with better terms than they had thought possible.

Yorktown dramatized the defeat of the most powerful of Old World nations, and, at least the beginning, too, of those three-century-old policies that regarded the American continents as legitimate spoils for European imperialism and mercantilism. But its significance was positive, not negative. It was not that it shattered an old empire, but that it called into existence a new one which its framers liked to call the "Empire of Reason." Soon Americans were drawing up the first written constitution, creating the first federal system, ending the ancient tyranny of colonialism, and introducing to politics the spectacle of a government that derived its authority from below, not above.

THE REVOLUTION VICTORIOUS. 1977. Oil on board, 18⅞x19⅝ in. Collection Mr. Homer Noble. "The red, white, and blue stripes of the flag strike an unusual note as Washington watches General Benjamin Lincoln accept the sword of surrender from the British."

46

Even before the American people declared their independence from the Mother Country, the Continental Congress appointed a committee to draft Articles of Confederation. The "drawing up" part was completed in 1779, but the states did not finally accept the new draft until 1781, so in fact the American states fought a revolution and won independence without a common government.

The Articles of Confederation themselves, admirable as they were both in principle and in detail, did not function very well. Indeed, with every year the central authority grew more impotent and the separate states more independent. Finally, under the leadership of Washington, Madison, and Hamilton, a call went out for a convention to amend the Articles so that they would be "adequate to the exigencies of Union." That convention met in Philadelphia in May 1787 and, after a little more than three months of debate, completed and signed the Constitution of the United States on September 17, 1787. After intensive and often heated debate, that constitution was ratified by the states and went into effect on April 16, 1789, when Washington took the oath of office and gave the first inaugural address in history.

That constitution has endured for two hundred years; it is now the oldest written constitution in history and, it is safe to say, the most successful. Indeed, it is difficult to challenge William Gladstone's tribute that "it is the most remarkable work in modern times to have been produced by the human intellect at a single stroke." It is also the most original, the most innovative, and, as it turned out, the most farsighted document of its kind. It was the first clearly democratic document of its kind in history, for it derived its authority from the people and was ratified by representatives of the people. It created the first workable federal system in history: one which has been a model to other nations throughout the globe. It was the first—on a national scale—to provide for separation of legislative, executive, and judicial authority, and to provide for the complete independence of the judiciary. It was the first—again excepting those written by the American states—to subordinate the military to the civil authority. It contained within itself provisions for expansion; and it did this not by adding colonies, as with Old World nations, but by providing for the admission of territories into states, which were

THE CONSTITUTION
DEBATED. 1985. Opaque
watercolor, 10⅜x12 in.
Collection of the artist.

WASHINGTON AT CARLISLE, 1794. 1989. Oil on canvas, 30x52 in. Collection U.S. Army War College, Carlisle, Pennsylvania.

then admitted to the Union on terms of absolute equality with the original states. It also contained the first Bill of Rights, which provided for substantive, as well as procedural rights, of all persons within its jurisdiction: thus, the new nation guaranteed freedom of religion, the separation of church and state, freedom of speech and of the press and of assembly.

In effect, the Constitution justified all three of those mottoes Franklin and Jefferson had selected as befitting the new United States: *E Pluribus Unum* (One in Many), *Annuit Coeptis* (God Has Favored Our Beginnings), and best of all *Novus Ordo Saeclorum* (A New Order of the Ages).

Nowhere in eighteenth-century Europe was there any genuine freedom of the press. In England, as late as 1789, Tom Paine was outlawed because his "Rights of Man" criticized the institution of the monarchy, and others were sentenced to exile in Botany Bay for daring to suggest the propriety of annual elections to Parliament. Even in the American colonies the exercise of freedom of the press was dangerous and uncertain—as Peter Zenger learned when he was jailed in 1735 (charged with seditious libel for criticizing Governor Crosby of New York) and as the Reverend Fysche Palamer learned when he was found guilty of treason and shipped off to Botany Bay for fourteen years. Yet Americans believed that the press should be free.

George Mason wrote a guarantee of freedom of the press into the first Virginia Constitution (indeed, it is to Virginia that we owe most for the vindication of this principle); John Adams soon followed with the same provision in the constitution of Massachusetts. Before long, most American state constitutions boasted that guarantee. At the very first session of Congress, James Madison drafted the Bill of Rights, which provided in its first article that "Congress shall make no law abridging the freedom of speech or of the press." Jefferson, too, thought this a "sacred principle." As he wrote Washington, "no government ought to be without censors and where the press is free none ever will"; elsewhere he observed that "were it left to me to decide whether we should have a government without newspapers or newspapers without a government, I should not hesitate a moment to prefer the latter." Thanks to the continued vindication of this principle of freedom of the press by the courts, Americans probably enjoy a greater degree of freedom of the press than do any other people.

LITTLE OLD NEW YORK. 1983. Oil on canvas, 28x34 in. Collection Chase Manhattan Bank.

In his farewell address, President Washington argued that "the great rule of conduct for us in regard to foreign nations is to have as little political connection as possible"; and that we should avoid "permanent, inveterate antipathies against particular nations and passionate attach-

ments for others." He spoke from experience, for during his second administration, "antipathies" and "attachments" had all but torn the nation apart. Confronted with the outbreak of revolution in France and its explosion into a war between that country and England, Washington had proclaimed "neutrality"—the first proclamation of its kind in history. But public opinion was deeply and even bitterly divided between the partisans of Revolutionary France—mostly followers of Jefferson—and those who feared the excesses of revolution and looked rather to Britain to preserve stability in the world. The conduct of the belligerents exacerbated these divisions; both great powers preyed on American commerce; and the British added affront to injury by refusing to surrender their military posts in the Northwest, as required by the Treaty of 1783. By the mid-1790s war seemed inevitable.

In this crisis Washington induced Chief Justice John Jay to sail to London to negotiate a settlement. What he brought home divided public opinion further: the Jeffersonians thought its terms an abject surrender, the Hamiltonians thought the avoidance of war worth almost any price. Washington threw his incomparable authority on the side of the treaty and managed to win a two-thirds vote in the Senate. The treaty was ratified on June 25, 1795, giving the new nation another fifteen or so years of breathing space in which to meet the crisis of 1812.

In one sense it can be said that the struggle for American independence did not come to an end until the War of 1812. It is not at all clear whether the Americans won that war on the battlefield or on the seas, but it is certain that they won it strategically, politically, and even philosophically. The American plan to invade and annex Canada was frustrated; the American capital was burned; the American navy and merchant marine were all but swept from the seas. Yet American victories in the Battle of Lake Erie and the Battle of Lake Champlain made clear that the British could not hope to recover any part of the Northwest, and the stunning defeat of the British at New Orleans—statistically the worst defeat in their history up to that time—enabled Americans to claim both military and moral superiority. After the Treaty of Ghent—ratified in February of 1815—not only Britain but all Europe left the United States strictly

NEGOTIATING THE JAY TREATY. 1976. Opaque watercolor, 14⅜x22⅛ in. Collection New York Bank for Savings.

Far right:
"SHALL I BOARD HER, SIR?" (USS *Constitution* vs HMS *Guerriere*, August 19, 1812). 1989. Oil on canvas, 34x50 in. Collection U.S. Marine Corps.

alone. Within a few years Monroe was to proclaim a
doctrine which in effect told Europe to keep its hands off
both of the American continents, and in time Americans
could believe that even this extreme Monroe Doctrine had
been vindicated by history.

The United States was born the largest nation in the New World. With the acquisition of Louisiana in 1803 and of the Floridas in 1812 and 1819, she more than doubled her original size. Could a nation as large as the whole of western Europe—which embraced over twenty nations—survive, or would the centrifugal forces of geography prove stronger than the centripetal forces of politics and sentiment? The answer to that most urgent question was to be found in the realms of economics, science, and technology —that is, in overcoming distance by effective transportation.

At the beginning of the century, Jefferson's Secretary of the Treasury, Gallatin, had proposed an elaborate network of roads and canals to knit together north and south, the Atlantic coast and the interior. The successful voyage of Robert Fulton's *Claremont* on the Hudson showed what could be accomplished by a network of rivers, lakes, and canals. De Witt Clinton, senator and governor of New York, early caught a vision of linking the Atlantic with the Great Lakes by a canal from the Hudson to Lake Erie; by 1817 he had persuaded the State of New York to undertake the stupendous task. Construction began on July 4, 1817; the canal reached Lake Erie at Buffalo in October of 1825. Three hundred sixty-five miles in length, it was, probably, the greatest engineering feat since the building of the Pyramids. Its significance was far-reaching: it assured New York the position of the greatest entrepot for the commerce of the West; it opened up the Old Northwest to a flood of emigration from New England and New York, and, thus, changed the character and culture of that area; and, by linking the Northwest economically with the Atlantic seaboard, it succeeded in diverting trade from the Ohio-Mississippi system, which fed into the south, to the north—a shift which assured, in the end, the support of that great area to the Union in the crisis of 1860.

The right of trial by a jury of peers—and by the law of the land—was guaranteed to every Englishman by the Magna Carta of 1215. This right of a fair trial—translated in our own constitution into the phrase "due process of law"—is one of the majestic concepts in the history of civilization. Until modern times, it was to be found only amongst English-speaking peoples. The English had carried it with them to their settlements in America, where it flour-

DEWITT CLINTON OPENS THE ERIE CANAL. 1976. Opaque watercolor, 14½x22 in. Collection New York Bank for Savings.
"There are virtually no contemporary pictorial accounts of this event upon which I could base my painting. We do know, however, that the boat was the *Seneca Chief* and that Governor Clinton's keg, now in the collection of the New York Historical Society, contained water from New York Harbor. These clues, plus portraits of Clinton, were the basis for my recreation of this scene."

FALL OF THE ALAMO. 1988.
Oil on canvas, 30x56 in.
Collection Mr. Craig Singer.

ished. The Americans wrote it into most of their state constitutions, and, by the fifth and sixth articles of the Bill of Rights, included it into the federal. Nor was the concept of a fair trial limited to provision for a jury of one's peers: the Bill of Rights also prohibited double jeopardy, cruel and unusual punishment, and self-incrimination; and specified that no one was to be deprived of life, liberty, or property without due process of law. To this guarantee the Fourteenth Amendment added that no state might "deny to any person within its jurisdiction the equal protection of the law"—a restriction only now taking on revolutionary significance.

From the beginning vast distances and limited means of transportation suggested that as the people could not all come to some capital city, judges should "ride circuit" and hold court in county centers. Thus, the first constitution of Ohio required that the supreme court judges should hold court in every county once a year. Holding court and conducting trials in the rural areas was often a homely affair, as Mr. Künstler has so aptly illustrated.

The first permanent English settlement in the New World was at Jamestown, in Virginia; but it is New England, rather than Virginia, that holds a special place in the American imagination. It is the pilgrim fathers we remember in song and story, not the first settlers at Jamestown

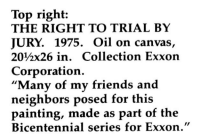

Top right:
THE RIGHT TO TRIAL BY JURY. 1975. Oil on canvas, 20½x26 in. Collection Exxon Corporation.
"Many of my friends and neighbors posed for this painting, made as part of the Bicentennial series for Exxon."

(with the exception of John Smith, to be sure, but he is remembered more for his romantic encounter with Pocahontas than for his attachment to the New World), and Thanksgiving is always in a New England setting. It is the New England town meeting that we conjure up as the model of democracy, not the county courts of the South. It is at Concord Bridge that minutemen fired the shot heard round the world, not at Great Bridge, Virginia. Faneuil Hall has somehow usurped the place of Bruton Church, and boys and girls in prairie towns proclaim with rapture their love for rocks and rills, for woods and templed hills.

The literary image, too, was formed by that galaxy of New England poets and novelists and historians whose visages once decorated the cards in the amiable game of Authors: Longfellow and Lowell, Whittier and Holmes, Emerson and Thoreau; and Walden, with only a few acres of water, became the best-known pond in America. It was the New Englanders, also, who wrote the histories that Americans read—from Bancroft and Prescott, Motley and Parkman to Henry Adams and, in our own day, Samuel Eliot Morison. It was Noah Webster of Connecticut who "invented" the American language; it was Horace Mann of Massachusetts who set the pattern for elementary education throughout the country. Here, Mr. Künstler, who has given us so many pictures of the plains and the Far West, pays tribute to New England.

No nation ever expanded as rapidly as the United States, or as vastly. How did it hold together? A network of roads, rivers, and canals, however elaborate, was wholly inadequate. The railroad—invented almost simultaneously in England and America—was the answer. George Stephenson was the steam-operated-locomotive pioneer in Britain, and his *Rocket* made a first run in 1825; John Stevens, an American, had anticipated the feat by a few months, but only by a trial run on his own estate. By the end of the 1820s a dozen projects were under way—the Baltimore and Ohio, the Charleston and Hamburg, the Mohawk and Hudson, the Boston and Lowell among them. The first to achieve success was that built by a group of South Carolina industrialists who formed a company to build tracks connecting Charleston with the Savannah River town of Hamburg. They laid down no less than 136 miles of track—the longest

THE LAMPLIGHTER. 1975.
Oil on illustration board,
20½x26 in. Collection Exxon
Corp.
"I used buildings from Old
Bethpage, Long Island, to
recreate this New England
scene. My son, David,
posed for the lamplighter."

railroad in the world at that time. In December 1830, *The Best Friend of Charleston* made its trial run on the newly built tracks; a few months later, a new and more powerful locomotive, the *West Point,* also pictured here, pulled out on a trial of speed, with barrier car and four cars for the 117 passengers—50 of whom were women.

Thereafter, railroad construction advanced with spectacular speed. By 1840, the new nation boasted 2,818 miles of track, by 1850 over 9,000, and by 1860 an astonishing 30,000—three times the mileage of Britain. It was to be of historical importance that most of this growth was in the Old Northwest: by 1860, Ohio alone had almost 3,000 miles of track, and Illinois, under the stimulus of lavish land grants from the federal government, some 2,800. A few years later a new breed of financiers and entrepreneurs were flinging tracks across the continent. On May 10, 1869, amidst national rejoicing, the tracks of the Union Pacific, building west from Omaha, and the Central Pacific, building east from California, were joined with a golden spike. It was a symbol of a reunited Union, reunited now East and West as well as North and South.

THE GOLDEN SPIKE. 1985. Opaque watercolor, 12x14 in. Collection Fleetwood, Division of Unicover Corp., Cheyenne, Wyoming.

Right:
THE FIRST AMERICAN STEAM LOCOMOTIVES. 1971. Oil on board, 30x40 in. Collection National Museum of American History, Smithsonian Institution, Washington, D.C. "This was one of the most difficult paintings I have done. I found the original blueprints of the *West Point* at the Engineers Society in New York. My research also took me to the B&O Museum in Baltimore, the Smithsonian Institution, and the site in Charleston. The building in the background still exists, but it has since gone through several additions and has been encompassed into the center of town."

III. THE FRONTIER

This picture of a "covered" wagon heading west while a locomotive powered train heads east illustrates four major themes of American history: the theme of the "significance of the frontier," or of open land; the theme of "mobility," physical and social alike; the theme of "freedom of travel," and the theme of the "industrial revolution," especially its overlapping phases. We take all four pretty much for granted; no inhabitant of eighteenth- or even early nineteenth-century Europe could do so. In the Old World

Page 63:
TOMAHAWK THROWING CONTEST (Detail).

Left:
MORNING MIST. 1981.
Oil on canvas, 30x40 in.
Collection of the artist.
"This painting captures the lighting effect of the mountains in British Columbia just before dawn. I tramped the streams in waders until I came upon this particular clump of driftwood, which worked perfectly with the painting's focal point, a mountain man whom I visualized as soon as I saw this spot."

Right:
THE MOVEMENT WEST. 1975. Oil on illustration board, 20¼x26 in. Collection Exxon Corp.

the passion for free or open land could be satisfied only by emigration to the New. There was open land in eastern Russia and Siberia, to be sure, but no right of migration from place to place or, for that matter, from job to job. Internal mobility in western European countries mostly found expression in forced abandonment of the land and movement into industrial cities. Most German states tried to prevent immigration to America, and even Britain placed restrictions on the emigration of certain skilled workers, such as Samuel Slater. Few Old World nations recognized the right of expatriation—a right which the United States always recognized and facilitated and which is now guaranteed in the United Nations Declaration of Human Rights. Finally,

where else could we find a better illustration of the elementary consideration that while the United States was, for a long while, considered a new and, in many respects, a primitive country, the whole of its national history lies within the confines of the Industrial Revolution.

Columbus had set out to find a short cut to the fabled Indies, and the fantasy of a "passage to India" lingered on for three centuries. Captain Cook had sought—in vain—such a passage on his famous voyage to the Pacific and Alaska in 1778; and Sir Alexander Mackenzie sought the same when he crossed Canada to the Pacific in the 1790s. The search was given new, if brief, life when Captain Robert Gray of Boston, returning from a voyage to China, discovered the great river he named after his ship, *Columbia*, in 1792.

It was in part to dispel this *ignis fatuus* that Thomas Jefferson—a scientist in his capacity as president of the American Philosophical Society, and a statesman in his capacity as President of the United States—decided to launch a great exploratory expedition across the continent to the Pacific coast. In January 1803, on the eve of the acquisition of the Louisiana Territory, he sought and obtained congressional approval for the enterprise.

To command the expedition he chose his secretary,

TOMAHAWK THROWING CONTEST. 1981. Oil on canvas, 36x54 in. Collection Mr. Robert E. Torray. "This painting depicts 'rendez-vous' for the mountain men, the time when they bring in their pelts to trade for supplies— and drink, carouse, and gamble. You can be sure there was many a bet riding on the toss of the tomahawk! I had a great deal of fun painting these trappers. There is nothing like a beard to add character to a face."

Right:
LEWIS AND CLARK. 1985. Opaque watercolor, 14½x20½ in. Collection Hammer Galleries, New York.

TOO LATE. 1985. Oil on canvas, 30x40 in. Collection Mr. John S. Davidson. "The idea of painting mountain men coming into a trading post shortly after an Indian raid was given to me over the phone by John S. Davidson, who, I am pleased to say, is the owner of the painting."

Captain Meriwether Lewis, and Captain William Clark, brother of the revolutionary hero George Rogers Clark. Jefferson himself prepared the agenda for the expedition: to find "the most direct and practical water communications to the Pacific"; to explore the mineral and other resources of the vast territory and report on its flora and fauna; to make precise records of temperature and other such scientific data as would be useful; and to gather material on Indian languages and customs—one of Jefferson's lifelong interests. What was implicit rather than explicit was to lay a foundation for American claims to the "Oregon" country—territory which the British had claimed themselves and which the Hudson's Bay Company already occupied.

During the winter of 1803–4 the members of the expedition, forty-eight strong, outfitted and trained at Saint Louis, Missouri. In May 1804 they set out on their great adventure, following the Missouri almost two thousand miles to its juncture with the Yellowstone, where they camped for the winter. The next spring, guided by the heroic Snake Indian squaw Sacajawea, they crossed the Continental Divide and from there made their way down the Clearwater River—clear, but turbulent—to the mighty Columbia and from there, aided by members of the friendly Nez Percé—the tribe the United States Army all but exterminated in 1877—reached the mouth of the Columbia. On the 7th of November, they first caught sight of the Pacific Ocean. A month later they reached it. Captain Clark carved on the trunk of a pinetree "By land from the United States, 1804 and 05," and in his journal he wrote, "reached Cape Disappointment at the entrance of the Columbia River to the Great South Sea and the Pacific Ocean." That brought to a triumphant close the heroic adventure launched in 1492 when Christopher Columbus informed King Ferdinand of Spain that "on the third of August I left Palos and stood out to sea."

In most of North America, it was the fur trade that opened up the continent, luring trappers and traders and explorers to every corner of the vast domain. French, Spanish, British, and Americans mingled with the Indians, precipitating fierce competition and, in the end, war.

The beginnings of that trade can be traced back to 1525, when a Portuguese navigator, Esteban de Gomez, returned home with a cargo of the "skins of wild beasts"; it was prophetic that his cargo also included some fifty Indians to be sold into slavery. By the beginning of the next century, the competition between great fur companies and the *coureurs de bois*, who devoted their lives to tracking down mink, beaver, otter, and fox—and the Indians who supplied them—raged in almost every quarter of the continent. The furs came cheap: the Indians could be fobbed off with a weapon, a string of beads, or more commonly, all the "firewater" they could drink. Transportation was easy along the

FRIENDS, OLD AND NEW. 1980. Oil on canvas, 26x20 in. Collection Mr. Bernard Haber.

Left:
NIGHT WATCH. 1981. Oil on canvas, 24x18 in. Collection Mr. T. G. Rogers.

Right:
NIGHT TRAIL. 1982. Oil on canvas, 16x20 in. Collection Mr. and Mrs. M. Demenus.
"This mountain man, using the cover of darkness to make his escape from unfriendly Indian territory, is undoubtedly hoping for fresh snowfall to hide his tracks."

rivers that flowed into the Atlantic; the markets almost limitless and profits immense. No wonder that almost one-third the population of French Canada was involved, in one way or another, in this trade.

The center of the trade was for a long time in the Saint Lawrence-Great Lakes area, long controlled by the French, in alliance with a score of Indian tribes. But by the late eighteenth century, the British had become dangerous rivals. Control of the lucrative trade was one of the major issues in the French and Indian War as it was, later, in the conflict between Britain and the new United States for the Old Northwest and again, a generation later, for the Oregon Country. While the "mountain men" and the *coureurs de bois* worked pretty much on their own, the trade itself drifted more and more into the hands of great companies: the Hudson's Bay Company, the American Fur Company, the Rocky Mountain, the Missouri, and others. By the dawn of the nineteenth century, their rivalry was like that of the great oil companies seeking for off-shore oil today—and their profits almost as dazzling.

Few commercial activities have played a larger role in history than the American fur trade. It was the fur trader who explored the continent, penetrating its most remote and

MOVING ON. 1983. Oil on canvas, 30x40 in. Collection Hammer Galleries, New York.
"Having trapped out the area, the mountain men have decided to move on to new territory—but not before the trapper in the foreground takes a last look for signs of beaver."

Right:
MAN AND HIS MOUNTAIN. 1982. Oil on canvas, 16x20 in. Collection Mr. Elisha Cohen.
"In this symbolic portrait, I deliberately enlarged this trapper's hands, which have been through so much wear and tear. Most trappers ended up with arthritis from all the years of setting traps in ice-cold streams."

inaccessable spaces, carving out trails through forests and mountain passes, mapping not only the geography but the resources of the continent, and, in the nineteenth century, setting up scores of forts and outposts both for convenience and defense. Successful trade depended on "cooperation" from Indians, cooperation bought not only by military alliances and by trading, but by exploiting, debauching, and killing off the native races.

The fur trade was a form of war, as well as of commerce: warfare between Indian tribes, between European powers, between the Old and the New Worlds, and, to some extent, between rival companies. From the foundation of the Hudson's Bay Company in the seventeenth century, the trade was an international business. With Captain Gray's voyage to China —bearing a cargo of furs from the Oregon Country—it moved into new and fabulously rich markets. The resultant "China Trade" helped create not only a new merchant aristocracy for enterprising shipbuilders and traders out of Salem and Boston, but opened doors to a new world of Chinese culture, silks, tea, and spices.

Even before the discovery of gold in California, the promise of a new life in a new land caused many men to pack up their families and move west. As the cost of passage by ship was prohibitive and the railroads had not yet linked East and West, they traveled in canvas-covered wagons, carrying as much of their household goods and supplies as they could. The journey was long and exhausting and full of danger. With barely discernible trails and constant fear of Indian attack, families joined wagon trains with reputable guides who could lead them safely across the plains and mountains. Yet even experienced wagon masters could not insure against drought, famine, and early snowfall. No story in our history excites more horror than that of the ill-fated Donner Party, which, in 1846, became trapped in the snowy Sierras and, as their food gave out and fellow travelers died, succumbed to cannibalism to keep alive.

The modern reader of such tales finds it difficult to believe that pioneers setting out so hopefully from Missouri to Oregon or California really understood the perils awaiting them; surely, if they had, they never would have started. Yet we should remember the state motto of California—"The

THE SINGER FAMILY. 1981. Oil on canvas, 36x48 in. Collection Mr. Craig Singer.

Left:
EMILY. 1983. Oil on canvas, 28x36 in. Collection Dunnegan Gallery of Art, Bolivar, Missouri.
"There were very few moments for quiet reflection moving west on a wagon train. Perhaps the rest of the pioneers are out on the prairie, possibly burying one of their own."

Right:
PRAIRIE SCHOONERS WEST. 1982. Oil on board, 22¾x30 in. Collection Mrs. Gertrude Spratlen.

cowards never started; the weak died on the way." The arduous nature of such travel is best described by one who lived and suffered through it. Listen to Sarah Royce, mother of philosopher Josiah Royce, who, in 1849, with her husband and baby daughter, made the trek across the continent in search of El Dorado. Her remembered reaction to learning that they were lost somewhere outside of Salt Lake City illustrates well the near hopelessness that could overtake such pioneers even when their passage was accomplished in relative safety:

> When the explorers returned from their walk to the ridge, it was only to report no discovery, nothing to be seen on all sides but sand and scattered sagebrush interspersed with the carcasses of dead cattle. So there was nothing to be done but to turn back and try to find the meadows. . . . Turn back, on a journey like that, in which every mile had been gained by the most earnest labor, growing more and more intense until of late it had seemed that the certainty of advance with every step was all that made the next step possible. In all that long journey no steps ever seemed so heavy, so hard to take, as those with which I turned my back to the sun that afternoon of October 4, 1849.

America was born of immigration and the American empire, with its limitless expanse of open land, invited further immigration. Mobility has been, from the beginning, perhaps the most deeply basic characteristic of the American people; we have always been "on the go," and we still are. No wonder travel and transportation have loomed large in our history and our imagination: Indian trails, the Wilderness Road, the Cumberland Gap, the Conestoga wagon, the *Claremont*, the flatboat, the Erie Canal, the Clipper ship, the Mississippi steamboat, the Sante Fe Trail, the Oregon Trail, the Pony Express, the stagecoach.

The problem of inland transportation took on new urgency when settlement leaped the 1,500-mile barrier from the Mississippi to the Pacific in the 1840s and 50s. Transportation around the Straits of Magellan or across the Isthmus of Panama was long and costly. There had to be some quicker way. Within a quarter century the railroads were to meet this challenge. In the meantime connection between the Mississippi-Missouri frontier and the West depended on the Pony Express and the stagecoach.

As early as 1857, the government contracted with John Butterfield to deliver mail to the mountainous west and the Pacific coast via El Paso and Yuma in Arizona. Proponents

THE PONY EXPRESS. 1985. Opaque watercolor, 8¼x9½ in. Collection Saks Galleries, Denver, Colorado.

Left:
MULE TRAIN. 1980. Oil on canvas, 22x28 in. Collection Mr. and Mrs. Vincent Bellitte.
"When the singer Frankie Lane saw a story about me in a magazine, he called me to suggest I do a painting depicting his big hit of the 1950s, 'Mule Train.' This is the result."

**EARLY MORN, LATE
START.** 1977. Oil on
canvas, 24x30 in. Collection
Mr. J. Bishop.

for a more direct route through Salt Lake City set up a rival express, which under the control of that Napoleon of the mountains, Ben Halladay, inaugurated a Pony Express which provided service twice a week to Salt Lake City and San Francisco. Meanwhile, beginning at the same time, the Overland Stage, with one hundred Concord coaches, eight hundred drivers, and fifteen hundred horses provided weekly service from Saint Louis to San Francisco in only twenty-five days, and at a cost of one hundred dollars—rather less than it costs today for a four-hour flight.

THE RACE BETWEEN THE NATCHEZ AND THE ROBERT E. LEE. 1985. Opaque watercolor, 12x16 in. Collection Hammer Galleries, New York.

Right:
THE RACE. 1984. Oil on canvas, 25x36 in. Collection Hammer Galleries, New York.

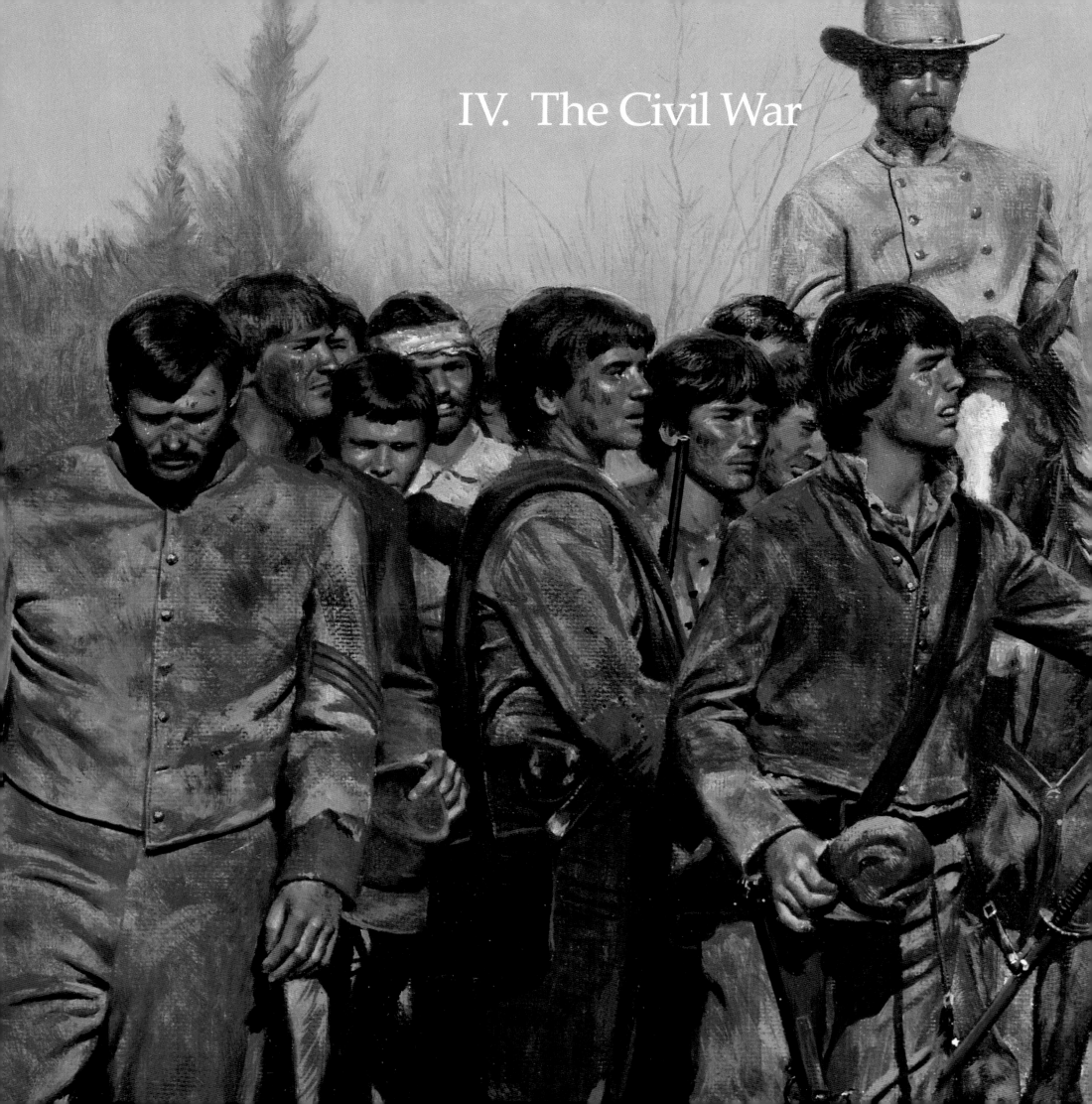

IV. The Civil War

IV. CIVIL WAR

As early as 1835 that most perspicacious of all observers, Alexis de Tocqueville, predicted (in his *Democracy in America*) that the Union would not survive: slavery, he asserted, would divide it. His prediction was vindicated when on December 20, 1860, South Carolina seceded from the Union. Most of the other slave states followed her out of the Union and, in March of 1861, formed The Confederate States of America. Virginia—the oldest and the most powerful of all the slave states, and the one with the strongest ties to the Union—held aloof.

Meantime South Carolina—and the new Confederate government—precipitated the issue and forced Virginia's hand, as it were, by insisting on the surrender of all Union forces on "Confederate" soil or in her waters. In late December 1860 and January 1861 Confederates seized forts and arsenals from Charleston to Florida, and from Baton Rouge to Arkansas and Texas. At this juncture Major Anderson, in command of Fort Moultrie in Charleston harbor, moved his garrison to Fort Sumter. Determined to bring Virginia into the Confederacy by an open break, General Beauregard, in command at Charleston, opened fire on the fort at the dawn of April 13. After thirty-four hours of intense, but bloodless, bombardment, Major Anderson surrendered. Lincoln declared that an insurrection existed and called for 75,000 volunteers; Virginia seceded; and the war was on.

In retrospect it is clear that whatever the immediate advantages of the reduction of Fort Sumter, the ultimate cost to the Confederacy was high. For while the opening of hostilities brought Virginia into the Confederacy, firing on Fort Sumter branded the Confederacy as the aggressor, and galvanized the North into defense of the Union and the flag. "There is among us," wrote Horace Binney of Philadelphia, "but one thought, one object, one end, one symbol—the Stars and Stripes."

Americans have fought eight major wars since the War for Independence; of them all, it is the Civil War—which Southerners persist in calling the War Between the States—that has left the most lasting impression on our history,

THE LINCOLN-DOUGLAS DEBATES. 1987. Oil on canvas, 30x30 in. Collection Mr. José Pires.
"The debates before the Civil War propelled Lincoln into national prominence. I placed Lincoln in the foreground to exaggerate his height of 6'4" in contrast to the 'Little Giant' who was only 5'3"."

Right:
"THERE STANDS JACKSON LIKE A STONE WALL" (Gen. Thomas J. Jackson, First Manassas, July 21, 1861). 1991. Oil on canvas, 24x36 in. Collection Dr. and Mrs. Barry George.
"A rather odd sight, in the first major battle of the war, was that of this Confederate officer in his pre-war blue uniform from Virginia Military Institute. Through the smoke of battle the first national flag of the newly formed Confederacy could easily be mistaken for the Stars and Stripes. It was here that Thomas J. Jackson, leading a Virginia brigade, stood 'like a stone wall' and earned his nickname and immortality."

FIRST TO THE GUNS (Battle of Wilson's Creek, Missouri, August 10, 1861). 1992. Oil on canvas, 18x30 in. Collection Dunnegan Gallery of Art, Bolivar, Missouri.
"In the first major battle of the western theater, a Louisiana brigade, carrying their state 'pelican' flag overran a federal artillery position and helped turn the tide into another victory for the South."

GHOST COLUMN (Col. Nathan Bedford Forrest, Fort Donelson, Tennessee, February 16, 1862). 1991. Oil on canvas, 22x30 in. Collection Mr. Kenneth Rosenberg.
"To center attention on Colonel Forrest, I deliberately did not show any other faces and utilized the snow-laden branches to lead the viewer's eye into the picture."

THE *MONITOR* AND THE *MERRIMACK* (Hampton Roads, Virginia, March 9, 1862). 1985. Oil on board, 12x14 in. Collection Mr. Joel Grey.

"In this first battle of ironclads, the *Monitor* would emerge victorious. However, neither the *Monitor* nor the *Merrimack* would survive the war. The research for this painting was done at the U.S. Navy Memorial Museum and the Smithsonian Institution."

our minds and our imaginations. It was the first modern war, the first to be fought with railroads and the telegraph and the balloon, and with torpedoes and ironclads. Of all our wars since the Revolution, it was perhaps the only one which achieved clear-cut objectives: it was fought to save the Union and end slavery, and it did both. It is Civil War songs we still hear—"Dixie Land," "Marching Through Georgia," and "The Battle Hymn of the Republic." It furnished the best war poetry: no other war has produced anything comparable to Whitman's "Drum Taps," or Melville's "Battle Pieces," or Lowell's "Harvard Commemoration Ode." It gave us our most cherished heroes—Lincoln and Lee, above all. Nor has any other war—not even the Revolution—contributed so much to our traditions and our folklore. Much of that folklore centers on Johnny Reb and Billy Yank, opponents who differed not at all in character or conduct. For the most part, they were boys drawn from farms and villages, volunteers and civilians at heart, but fighting with desperate courage for the Union or for "Southern Rights."

With these paintings, Mr. Künstler joins the long list of American artists and authors who have paid tribute to those who fought in the Civil War.

Above, left:
WAR BETWEEN THE STATES. 1956. Opaque watercolor. 17x14½ in. Collection Mr. George Tyler.

Above, right:
STILL FLYING. 1982. Opaque watercolor. 17x14½ in. Collection Mrs. William Ford.
"This was done as a mate to *War Between the States*, though it was painted twenty-six years later."

Right:
FIGHT AT FALLEN TIMBERS (Forrest and Morgan at Shiloh, April 8, 1862). 1991. Oil on canvas, 22x36 in. Collection Hammer Galleries, New York.
"In this wild charge against Union infantry, Forrest ended up alone and behind enemy lines. He was badly wounded in the melee but somehow managed to cut his way out and make it back to the safety of his own forces."

UNTIL WE MEET AGAIN
(Jackson's Headquarters,
Winchester, Virginia, Winter
1862). 1990. Oil on canvas,
30x46 in. Collection F&M
Bank, Winchester.
"Jackson's wife, Mary Ann,
would often bring him supper
in a basket. The building still
exists, somewhat changed, but
well preserved and serving the
public as a museum."

Right, above:
"RAISE THE COLORS AND
FOLLOW ME!" (Irish Brigade
at Antietam, September 17,
1862). 1991. Oil on canvas,
30x44 in. Collection U.S.
Army War College, Carlisle,
Pennsylvania.
"On walking the terrain at
Antietam battlefield, it is hard
to believe the extraordinary
courage shown by the Irish
Brigade in their headlong
charge into the withering fire
of the well-entrenched enemy."

Right:
MORGAN'S RAIDERS
(Alexandria, Tennessee,
December 21, 1862). 1982. Oil
on canvas, 25x40 in. Collection
Mr. William R. Frist.
"On one of the more daring
raids of the war, the
'Christmas' raid into Kentucky
was led by Gen. John Hunt
Morgan. He wreaked havoc
upon Union railroads, bridges,
and supplies and, in general,
terrorized the state's citizens."

THE LAST COUNCIL
(Jackson, Lee, and Stuart at Chancellorsville, May 1, 1863). 1990. Oil on canvas, 28x36 in. Collection Mr. and Mrs. Arnold Gumowitz.
"Showing the light source is always dramatic for a painting. However, I found the completely exposed fire too distracting and covered most of it with the pots in the foreground. This would be the last council of Lee and Jackson. The next day, 'Stonewall' was mortally wounded, mistakenly shot by his own men."

Top, left:
EMANCIPATION PROCLAMATION. 1987. Oil on canvas, 30x30 in. Collection Mr. and Mrs. Michael L. Sharpe.
"In doing the research for this painting, I worked from the notes of Francis B. Carpenter who was given access to the White House and actually had Lincoln pose for him. The table, chairs, rug, and even the wallpaper are accurate. I naturally silhouetted Lincoln against the light of the window to have the viewer focus on the center of interest: the president."

Bottom, left:
COL. ROBERT GOULD SHAW AND THE 54TH MASSACHUSETTS (Boston, May 28, 1863). 1991. Oil on canvas, 16x20 in. Collection Hammer Galleries, New York.
"The first black volunteer regiment of the war, the 54th Massachusetts became a model of perfection and drill in camp. They valiantly attacked Fort Wagner on the South Carolina coast, led by Col. Robert Gould Shaw who was killed in the assault. Although the attack failed and they suffered 50 percent casualties, the regiment fought courageously."

THE GRAND REVIEW
(Brandy Station, Virginia, June 5, 1863). 1989. Oil on canvas. 28x44 in. Collection Mr. and Mrs. Frank B. Gilbreth. "This was the high point of the Confederate cavalry. I tried to show the pomp and pageantry of the moment. As they rode to a formal ball that evening, Gen. J. E. B. Stuart's cavalry seemed invincible. Four days later, they were attacked by Union cavalry at Brandy Station; the aura about them would never be the same."

Top, left:
LEE AND STAFF (Gettysburg).
1993. Opaque watercolor,
17x13⅝ in. Collection
Hammer Galleries, New York.

Bottom, left:
CHAMBERLAIN'S CHARGE
(Col. Joshua Lawrence
Chamberlain, Little Round
Top, July 2, 1863). 1994. Oil
on canvas, 20x32 in. Collection
Hammer Galleries, New York.
"I used the dappled sunlight
streaming through the trees to
focus attention on one of the
great warriors of the Civil War,
Col. Joshua Lawrence
Chamberlain, during his
famous and heroic charge
down Little Round Top at
Gettysburg."

Above:
"HOLD AT ALL COSTS!"
(Gen. John Buford, Gettysburg,
July 1, 1863, 9:30 A.M.). 1993.
Opaque watercolor, 12½x36⅞ in.
Collection Hammer Galleries,
New York.
"Union Gen. John Buford's
cavalry brigade was the first to
make contact with the
Confederate army at
Gettysburg. He had his
dismounted forces hold a
defensive position against
overwhelmingly superior
numbers, giving precious time
for the Union army to come up
and take defensive positions
on the 'high ground.'"

"IT'S ALL MY FAULT" (Gen.
Robert E. Lee, Gettysburg,
July 3, 1863). 1989. Oil on
canvas, 26x48 in. Collection
Mr. Thorne Donnelly, Jr.
"With the repulse of Pickett's
charge, Lee himself met the
dazed survivors and blamed
himself for the defeat. I used
the dead tree and branches to
set the mood of devastation
and defeat."

THE HIGH TIDE (Gettysburg, July 3, 1863). 1993. Opaque watercolor, 16x28¾ in. Collection Mr. George Kellner. "At the stone wall on Cemetery Ridge, the Confederate forces briefly broke through the Union line before they were pushed back. It is known to this day as the 'High Water Mark' of the Confederacy and is so marked at the national military park."

THE GLORIOUS FOURTH
(Gen. Ulysses S. Grant,
Vicksburg, July 4, 1863). 1989.
Oil on canvas, 34x56 in.
Collection Mr. and Mrs.
Michael L. Sharpe.
"This is, without doubt, the
most difficult painting I have
ever done. After months of
work, I finally finished the
picture on July 4, 1989. It is
the only painting I have ever
dated with the month and day.
With all the effort I expended,
when I finally finished the
piece, it was truly a glorious
Fourth for me."

Top:
BATTLE ABOVE THE CLOUDS (Lookout Mountain, Tennessee, November 24, 1863). 1992. Oil on canvas, 22x35 in. Collection Hammer Galleries, New York.
"While walking the battlefield of Lookout Mountain in Chattanooga, I searched for a distinctive boulder until I found this grouping. It existed during the battle just as it does today."

Bottom, left:
ULYSSES S. GRANT. 1990. Oil on board, 10x11½ in. Collection Hammer Galleries, New York.

Bottom, right:
ROBERT E. LEE. 1991. Oil on board, 10x11½ in. Collection Hammer Galleries, New York.

THE GETTYSBURG ADDRESS (November 19, 1863). 1987. Oil on canvas, 30x30 in. Collection Mr. and Mrs. Harold Bernstein.
"I am delighted that the National Park Service requested this image for a poster."

Top, left:
ON TO RICHMOND (Grant in the Wilderness, May 7, 1864). 1991. Oil on canvas, 30x42 in. Collection U.S. Army War College, Carlisle, Pennsylvania. "In some of the most horrible fighting of the war, where many of the wounded were burned to death by fires, the Union soldiers cheered their commander when they realized that he was marching southward and not north in defeat. To bring the viewer's eye to Grant, I placed him and his black hat against the bright light of the still-burning fires in back of him."

Bottom, left:
BRINGING CLEBURNE HOME (Franklin, Tennessee, December 1, 1864). 1991. Oil on canvas, 24x36 in. Collection Hammer Galleries, New York.
"The Battle of Franklin was a devastating defeat for the Confederacy. I tried to tell this story in the most direct way possible—by showing the horrors of war with lots of bodies. I used the early morning sun to focus attention on Cleburne as all eyes are on him. But the eye finally comes to rest on the shadowy foreground and delivers the real message."

Right:
"WAR IS HELL!" (Gen. William Tecumseh Sherman, Atlanta, November 15, 1864). 1991. Oil on canvas, 30x38 in. Collection Mr. Kenneth Rosenberg.
"What better way to show 'Uncle Billy' than silhouetted against the fire with the stark shapes of 'Sherman's Sentinels,' the burned-out chimneys of Atlanta."

"WE STILL LOVE YOU, GENERAL LEE" (Appomattox Court House, Virginia, April 9, 1865). 1992. Oil on canvas, 54x88 in. Collection Hammer Galleries, New York.
"I once read how, after the surrender at Appomattox Court House, General Lee rode back through his troops. Word of the surrender had already spread, and he was met with great sorrow. According to that account, some soldiers 'reached out to touch his horse as he rode by.' The title of this painting comes from that same account."

108

HER NAME WAS
SOJOURNER TRUTH. 1977.
Oil on board, 20¾x17½ in.
Collection Deborah A.
Künstler.
"My wife was the model for
this idealized version of a
young Sojourner Truth. The
only known photograph of
Sojourner Truth shows her as
an elderly woman. I gave
Debbi this painting just before
my first show at the Hammer
Galleries."

Right:
ABRAHAM LINCOLN. 1991.
Oil on board, 10x11⅜ in.
Collection Hammer Galleries,
New York.

"I tremble for my country," wrote Thomas Jefferson of slavery when he was Governor of Virginia, "when I reflect that God is just; that his justice cannot sleep forever. . . . The whole commerce between master and slave is a perpetual exercise of the most boisterous of passions, the most unremitting despotism on the one part, the most degrading submissions on the other. . . . This abomination must have an end, and there is a superior bench reserved in Heaven for those who hasten it." Mostly it is the white leaders of abolitionism like John Jay or Owen Lovejoy, William Lloyd Garrison or Theodore Parker, who have been conceded that superior bench in Heaven; the contribution of the blacks themselves has been neglected. Yet men and women like Frederick Douglass; James Pennington; Joshua Henson (who may have been the original of Uncle Tom); David Ruggles, head of the New York Vigilance Committee; Dr. Martin Delany, who had studied medicine at Harvard and contributed richly to anti-slavery literature; Charlotte Forten of Philadelphia; Harriet Tubman, known as "Moses" for her work on the "underground railroad"; and Sojourner Truth, born Isabella Baumfree, the subject of this symbolic portrait, were not insignificant in furthering the cause of abolition.

Isabella Baumfree had been born in New York at a time when slavery was still legal. The state Emancipation Act of 1827 freed her, and it was then she adopted the name by which she is known and celebrated. A self-styled prophetess and itinerant preacher, she was accepted by leading abolitionists like Lucretia Mott, the Grimke sisters, and Harriet Beecher Stowe. After the Civil War she continued to be active in the struggle for Negro rights, guaranteed in the Constitution, but ignored or flouted by North and South alike; in the process she became the first black to win a slander suit against a white citizen and was instrumental in desegregating public transportation in the national capital.

In the American Valhalla, Abraham Lincoln occupies a special place. He is, certainly in our own day, the only man to be a hero to most of the world. He is, too, one of the few whose apotheosis is based not so much on his achievements—momentous as these were—but on his character. He was, even in his lifetime, known not so much as president or as commander-in-chief of great armies, but quite simply as Father Abraham; and the monuments which

have been erected to him, both artistic and literary, show him not in power or in triumph, but brooding over the trials of mankind, or leaning over to bless little children he has saved from a life of slavery.

Born in a log cabin on a hardscrabble Kentucky farm, Lincoln grew to maturity in frontier Indiana and Illinois; it was he who gave vitality to the "log cabin" myth of American politics—only with him much that seemed myth was reality. How Lincoln emerged from obscurity to state, and then to national fame, is forever a puzzle. His literary style he learned from the Bible, which, we may assume, taught him a noble eloquence and compassion; his law from Joseph Story's *Commentaries of the Constitution*, which voted for nationalism on every page; and his politics from Jefferson, who taught magnanimity, and from Daniel Webster, who taught the sanctity of the Union at any cost. These were the qualities he displayed in those famous debates with Senator Douglas in 1858—debates that brought Lincoln not only national fame, but national respect.

The rest is history. His election was followed by the secession of eleven southern states; Lincoln stood firm in his determination that the Union must be preserved whatever the cost; and then the war came. In the course of that tragic struggle, Lincoln became convinced that the Union could not survive half slave and half free, and he freed the slaves. He conducted the fierce Civil War with wisdom, courage, shrewdness, and magnanimity, and when it ended the Union was once more intact.

Re-elected to the presidency, Lincoln said, in the noblest address in our history, "let us judge not that we be not judged," and called upon the people to harbor "malice toward none, charity for all." Less than six weeks later he died, as the lilacs bloomed, struck down by a fanatic Confederate, actor John Wilkes Booth.

"Now," said Seward, "he belongs to the ages." But Secretary Welles, who was there, put it best: "In front of the White House hundreds of colored people, mostly women and children, were weeping and wailing their loss. Their great benefactor was dead. Their hopeless grief affected me more than anything else."

V. THE WEST

Perhaps the most remarkable feature of American history is its telescopic quality. Changes, transformations, which in the Old World took centuries, in America overlap, as it were: thus the swift transition from wilderness to civilization, from a primitive to a highly sophisticated culture, from the overlapping of frontiers—the white and the Indian, the agricultural and the hunting, the industrial and the agricultural; thus, the overlapping, too, of ethnic groups—the English, the Irish, the German, the Swedish, the Italian, the Polish, the Negro and the Jewish and the Oriental. An awareness of the transitory character of any American experience permeated Owen Wister's novel *The Virginian*, perhaps the most popular novel in the first decade of the twentieth century. We do not think of Virginians as cattlemen, nor would we expect the recreation of frontier Wyoming to come from a Philadelphia aristocrat, educated at Harvard and in Paris. Neither would we expect such a novel to be dedicated to that Knickerbocker aristocrat,

Page 113:
NEW GIRLS IN TOWN (Detail).

Left:
PACKING INTO THE BIG HORN. 1985. Oil on canvas, 20x28 in. Collection Hammer Galleries, New York.

Right:
BIG HORN RENDEZVOUS. 1985. Oil on canvas, 22x30 in. Collection Hammer Galleries, New York.
"My good friend Lou Frederick, who took me across the Big Horn, posed for me at Florence Pass. I used the snow in the background as a foil to draw the eye to the center of interest."

THE KANSAN. 1973. Oil on board, 33x26 in. Collection Dr. Siegfried Rosenbaum.
"This painting was used as the cover illustration for a book called *The Kansan*, although the tree and rocks are actually from the area around Cody, Wyoming."

**EARLY START. 1984. Oil
on canvas, 20x26 in.
Collection Hammer Galleries,
New York.**

Theodore Roosevelt. But Owen Wister lived in Wyoming, and Roosevelt was himself, for a while, a cattle rancher in the Dakota country.

Wister draws our attention to the transitory nature of so much of the American experience by his description of his own novel. It depicts "a vanished world. No journeys save those which memory can take, will bring you to it now. The mountains are there, and the infinite earth, and the air that seems forever the eternal fountain of youth—but where is the buffalo and the wild antelope and where the horseman with his pasturing thousands? So like his old self does the sage brush seem when revisited, that you wait for the horseman to appear. But he will never come again. He rides in his historic yesterday. You will no more see him gallop out of the unchanging silence than you will see Columbus on the unchanging sea. . . . What has become of the horseman, the cow puncher, the last romantic figure upon our soil?" What indeed, but that he now lives in the imagination of the novelist, the film producer, and the painter.

The great naturalist the Comte de Buffon wrote that "the horse is the proudest conquest of Man." He was also the most valuable. Certainly no other animal has so caught

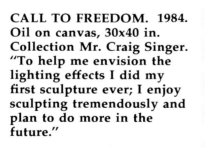

CALL TO FREEDOM. 1984.
Oil on canvas, 30x40 in.
Collection Mr. Craig Singer.
"To help me envision the lighting effects I did my first sculpture ever; I enjoy sculpting tremendously and plan to do more in the future."

CALL TO FREEDOM. 1984.
Bronze sculpture, 9x13½ in. with 10½ in. base.
Edition of 20.

the imagination. The Greeks imagined a creature half-horse, half-man—the Centaur—and when the Aztecs first saw Cortez mounted on his horse, they took him for a centaur. Not only ancient kings, but modern conquerors like the Duke of Wellington were buried with their horses; and General Robert E. Lee's Traveller is almost as famous as his master. No wonder: no other animal has served man so well in as many capacities. He has ploughed the fields, carried his master into battle, provided speedy transportation for men and goods, followed game for food and recreation; he has been the instrument of invasions and of conquests and the basis for changing economies.

The horse may have existed in the New World during the Pleistocene Era, but had died out long before the "discovery" of America by Europe. The Spanish *conquistadores* brought the horse with them—the Moorish horse, descendant of the Arabian, and the strongest and fleetest in the world. Soon they spread from the islands of the Caribbean to Mexico, and perhaps to Florida; northward into New Mexico and the Great Plains; and northward and westward into California. By the close of the seventeenth century, they had already transformed the economy of the Indians of the Plains and the mountains, and had created, in effect, a new culture—a culture based on hunting the buffalo and on war.

American frontiersmen, too, as they pushed steadily westward, were dependent on the horse. On each successive frontier, the horse played a decisive role: the frontier of exploration and hunting; the frontier of mining; the military frontier; and, above all, the cattleman's and sheepherder's frontier. Imagine the cowboy without his horse! No wonder horse theft was regarded by most westerners as a capital crime.

WILD HORSE MESA. 1982. Oil on canvas, 26x34 in. Collection Mr. Frank Dickstein. "I got up before sunrise to watch the round-up of these horses at the A Bar A ranch outside Saratoga, Wyoming."

The Sioux, whose hunting grounds ran from Minnesota to Montana and from the Canadian border to the Platte, were one of the most numerous, powerful, and warlike of all Indian nations. Though Lewis and Clark had described them in their journals, white Americans had few contacts with them before the settlement of the Minnesota country in the 1850s and the building of the transcontinental railroads through their lands in the next two decades. Thereafter—because of the decimation of the buffalo and the steady erosion of their hunting grounds by farmers and cattlemen—the contacts were mostly those of war. No chapter in the long and tragic history of the relations of white Americans with Indians symbolizes more dramatically our changing attitudes toward this story—the shift, that is, from prejudice and hostility to respect and guilt—than that which embraces Custer's Last Stand of 1876 and the Battle of Wounded Knee of 1890.

Seventy-five years ago no painting was more popular than one depicting, in lurid colors, Custer's Last Stand—the massacre by the Sioux, under Sitting Bull and Crazy Horse, of General Custer and all 264 of his men, at the battle of

Left:
CHIEF HIGH HORSE. 1985.
Oil on canvas, 20x16 in.
Collection Hammer Galleries,
New York.
"This is one of two
paintings I made of High
Horse, and one of a series of
portraits I did as the result
of a trip to the Rosebud
Sioux Reservation in South
Dakota during the summer
of 1984."

Above:
PAINTED HORSE. 1981.
Oil on canvas, 20x16 in.
Collection Mr. Harold
Bernstein.
"An aptly-titled painting,
this pictures a 'pinto' or
'paint' that is actually
painted as well. The Plains
Indians painted themselves
and their horses before
going into battle; each had
his own distinctive colors
and designs, believed to give
him mystical powers.
'Painted Horse' could also be
the name of this Sioux
warrior."

Right:
GOING FOR THE BIG
BULL. 1978. Oil on canvas,
26x34 in. Collection Mr.
and Mrs. Joseph A. Berger.

Little Big Horn—for it exhibited in gory detail the savagery of these fierce Plains Indians. What we remember today is rather Wounded Knee—the cold-blooded massacre of some two hundred Sioux men, women, and children by Colonel Forsyth and the seventh cavalry, because they refused to surrender their guns. It was a dusty culmination of A Century of Dishonor. No wonder Americans in the 1970s took to heart the line from Stephen Vincent Benet, "Bury my heart at Wounded Knee."

The Cheyenne, like the Sioux and other Plains Indians, depended on the buffalo for subsistence. Unlike the white hunters who came poaching on their lands, they did not kill merely for the precious pelts or the choice bits of meat. While the Indian, too, prized a warm buffalo robe, he never left the landscape dotted with carcasses rotting in the sun. Being nonagricultural, the Plains Indian needed the buffalo's flesh as the major staple in his diet; from the animal's hide, he fashioned not only his clothing, but his shelter—the conical tepee—and even an implement of war—his shield; from the bones and horns, he crafted cooking and eating utensils; from the sinews came his thread and bowstrings. The decimation of the buffalo that fol-

Left:
THE CHASE. Oil
on canvas, 16x20 in.
Collection Mr. James Fox.

Right:
THE TRAIL THAT LEAVES
NONE. 1983. Oil on
canvas, 28x36 in. Collection
Mr. L. Frederick.

lowed white "advancement" in the region threatened the Indian with extinction as well. The buffalo, once so vast in numbers that early pioneers reported it took days to pass a single herd—General Sheridan, as late as 1866, estimated that over one hundred million of them roamed the Plains—had dwindled by the late 1880s to, perhaps, not more than a thousand. Organized in 1905, the American Bison Society sought to save the buffalo, and since then there has been a gradual reversal, with herds being built up, especially in the Dakotas. Yet, such concern for the buffalo came too late to save the native culture of the Plains.

While numerous and warlike, the Plains Indians lacked the unity essential to effective resistance against American encroachment. The buffalo culture made hunting bands, rather than tribes, the most important social unit, and precluded large scale warfare. The beginnings of the decimation of the buffalo would pit Sioux against Cheyenne, Cheyenne against Arapaho, Arapaho against Pawnee in the attempt to survive. Overzealous soldiers and settlers like Colonel John Chivington and the Colorado Volunteers—responsible for the 1864 massacre of over 150 peaceful Cheyenne, awaiting supplies at Sand Creek, Colorado, before returning to their reservation—would give the Indian common cause and inflame his will to resist, but lack of traditional unity and leadership would make his efforts hopeless. Indian "victories" such as the Battle of Little Big Horn would be few; "defeats" such as those of Sand Creek and Wounded Knee were more the order of the day.

SURPRISE ATTACK. 1979. Oil on canvas, 30x40 in. Collection Mr. John S. Davidson.
"I attempted in this painting to capture the color, excitement, and action of a Sioux war party. The circle painted around the horse's eye was a common design, thought to give him exceptional sight in battle. The lead warrior carries a 'battle flag.'"

One of the most dramatic shifts in the kaleidoscope of American history was the replacement of millions of buffalo on the Great Plains by cattle, and of the Indian and the miner by the cowboy and the cattle king. The territory between the Missouri and the Rockies, and from Texas to the Canadian border—an area comprising one-fourth of the United States—was the cattle kingdom, the last and most picturesque American frontier.

The development of the cattle kingdom—and its unique culture, economy and society—in the 1870s and 80s was due to a peculiar combination of factors: the opening up of the public domain, the elimination of serious dangers from the Indians, the annihilation of the buffalo, the extension of railroads into the high plains, rapid increases in population at home and abroad which in turn increased beef consumption, the invention of the refrigerator car, and the growth of great packing centers in Chicago, Saint Louis, and Kansas City.

As early as 1856, a drove of Texas Longhorns had pastured their way to Chicago, but it was not until the late 1860s that the "long drive" became an institution. Cattlemen like Charles Goodnight and Jesse Chisholm marked out

Left:
AFTER THE RAIN. 1981.
Oil on board, 22¾x30 in.
Collection Mr. Howard M.
Bender.

Right:
HOME, HOME ON THE RANGE. 1983. Oil on canvas, 28x36 in. Collection of the artist.

trails on which thousands of herds beat a path sometimes a quarter mile broad. Altogether over six million cattle were driven north along these trails.

The cattle boom reached its peak in the mid-eighties. By that time it had ceased to be a frontier enterprise and had become pretty much a corporate business, organized and capitalized in the East and in England and Scotland. Meantime the hazards of ranching, both natural and man-made, were increasing enormously. The rapid fencing in of the open domain by "nesters," the appearance of cattle diseases which spread rapidly on the open range, and the enactment of state and territorial quarantine laws, the conflict between cattlemen and sheepherders and between cattlemen and the farmers, the precipitous decline of prices because of overproduction, the erosion of grasses on the open range from overgrazing, all presaged the decline of the cattle kingdom. Then came the two terrible winters of 1885–86 and 1886–87, which all but annihilated the herds.

RIDING POINT. 1982. Oil on canvas, 20x16 in. Collection Mr. Steven Adams.
"The cowboy's life was not a comfortable one: extreme heat, cold, dust, rain, snow, stampedes, and river crossings were daily travails. At least this hand is having a relatively easy time; the men riding drag will be eating dust all day."

Left:
LIGHTNING STAMPEDE. 1981. Oil on canvas, 16x20 in. Collection Mr. Stephen Wallace.
"Stampedes, a cowboy's worst fear, could start from something as insignificant as a cough and go on for days. Thunderstorms, a frequent cause of stampedes, were a constant danger."

EARLY CROSSING. 1978.
Oil on canvas, 24x36 in.
Collection Mr. John S.
Davidson.
"Although the water looks
calm here, this painting
depicts one of the most
potentially dangerous
moments of a cattle drive."

The blizzard of January 1877 was the worst ever known by cattlemen. Howling winds piled up immense snow drifts, and as the temperature fell to sixty-eight below zero, cattle pawed in vain through the frozen snow for grass, or fought to strip bark from the willows and the cottonwoods; thousands of cattle piled up against drifts or fences while other thousands died plunging into ravines and river bottoms to escape the icy blasts. That winter, in large part, wrote *finis* to the open range. Small cattlemen went under, and even the great corporations gave up and turned to more profitable investments. Something of the toll of nature and of man can be read in the history of Wyoming, where the number of cattle declined from nine million to three million in a single decade.

Left:
THE PRISONER. 1980. Oil on canvas, 24x34½ in. Collection Mr. John S. Davidson.

Right:
SUNDOWN POSSE. 1983. Oil on canvas, 24x30 in. Collection Mr. Vernon R. Drwenski.

Though the cattle kingdom collapsed by 1890 it left a lasting impact on the American popular imagination—an appeal to which a vast body of fiction, film, and television still caters. It is not surprising that Theodore Roosevelt should have ranched in the Badlands of Dakota, that Franklin Roosevelt's favorite song was "Home on the Range," or that President Eisenhower's favorite reading was Westerns.

Justice in the Wild West was a far cry from justice in the civilized East—though not, perhaps, in the violent South. Men were lured to the last frontier by the hope of riches; many, impatient with more conventional means, attempted to speed up the process by relieving others of their cattle, horses, gold, and even their lives. A violent society called for swift and violent justice. Sheriffs were appointed and courts convened; but jails were insecure and impartial juries often impossible to find. Most often, guilt or innocence was decided by the classic "shoot-out" on Main Street. Indeed, many of the lawmen in the West were chosen because of their reputations—deserved or not—as gunslingers: their only credentials were the notches on their guns, which served as the most effective detriment to crime.

Writers from the East roamed the West in search of
material to thrill and entertain their audiences at home.
They found what they sought in dubious "heroes" like
James Butler "Wild Bill" Hickock—gunslinger, buffalo
hunter, army scout, professional gambler and occasional U.S.
Marshall. The dime novelists of the late nineteenth century
and the filmmakers of the twentieth glorified the exploits of
men like "Wild Bill," who, if they were on the right side of
the law, appear to have been so by accident, rather than by
choice. Not so fortunate were those individuals who, while
also seeming to welcome the opportunity to reduce the
number of "badmen," did so for the rewards for their capture, "Dead or Alive." Bountyhunting is a time-honored
practice in America (the English paid the Indians for American scalps; early settlers in Arizona paid each other for
Apache scalps) but never quite respectable. To stand up to
an outlaw in a duel, even to shoot him in the back—the
rumored method of dispatch for "Wild Bill's" first vic-
tim—could be lauded, if the only gain was survival or
glory. To shoot a criminal in cold blood for money could
not. Thus we have Bob Ford, an ex-follower of the legendary Jesse James, who forgot past loyalties in the face of future reward and shot his former leader, becoming im-
mortalized in a popular ballad as "that dirty little coward . . .
[who] laid poor Jesse in his grave."

Left:
BRINGING IN GERONIMO.
1981. Oil on canvas, 25x34
in. Collection Mr. and Mrs.
M. Demenus.

Right:
DANGEROUS CROSSING.
1981. Oil on board, 17x22¾
in. Collection Mr. William
and Dr. Joyce Harlin.

Long before the Americans moved into the Southwest, the warlike character of the region's Indians was well established. It was a necessary attribute of bands of hunters and gatherers in constant competition for the meager livelihood that the deserts allowed. Those who did not fight, did not survive. One of the fiercest of the southwestern nations was the Apache. Inhabitants of Arizona and New Mexico and lands south of the border, as well, the Apaches were divided into many tribes, and often warred against each other. Splendid horsemen—Apache war ponies could cover nearly one hundred miles per day—they became masters of the hit-and-run tactics. Their small, expert bands were all that were needed to keep first the Spanish and later the Mexicans from settling in the lands they claimed as their own. Then the Americans came. Apache land—most of it arid and barren—was not desired by the farmer, but free access to the gold and agricultural fields of California was deemed necessary by settlers and soldiers alike.

The Apaches were amongst the last to accept American domination: the Chiricahua, under the leadership of the dread Geronimo, continued the struggle until 1886. Yet in the end all of the proud "savages" who had once ruled the continent were settled on inhospitable government reservations, cut off from the free life to which they had been accustomed for centuries, disintegrating culturally and physically—tragic reminders of the race that had helped the white man to adjust himself to the New World. Chief Joseph of the Nez Percé, at the end of his vain attempt to escape such a fate, could speak for most of them:

> I am tired of fighting. Our Chiefs are killed. . . . It is cold and we have no blankets. The little children are freezing to death. . . . My heart is sick and sad. I am tired.

HIS NEW BLUE COAT. 1977. Oil on canvas, 20x16 in. Collection Mr. Joel Grey.
"Though it is torn, dirty, worn, and taken from a fallen cavalryman, to this Apache warrior this is a new blue coat — and a great find."

Right:
APACHE FEET LEAVE NO TRACKS. 1983. Oil on canvas, 25x32 in. Collection Mr. Douglas R. Phillips.
"The Apache had an incredible ability to survive in the wild, aided by his knack of seemingly blending into the scenery."

For the majority of Americans, Indian history ends with the surrender of Geronimo in 1886. The battles are over, the bloodthirsty savage is vanquished; what more is there to know? The last two decades have witnessed a slight resurgence of popular interest in the Indian, sparked by the media's overexposure of events such as the 1969 "capture" of Alcatraz or the reckless occupation of Wounded Knee, South Dakota, by the radical American Indian Movement in 1973; but such interest is tinged with not a little irritation. Indian activism of this type, while not unnoticed, is hardly appreciated by the American public. Neither are the well-publicized claims to lands, held privately, in Massachusetts and elsewhere. Unhappily, the quieter activism of such groups as the National Congress of American Indians and the century-long disintegration of Indian culture which they seek to combat rarely make headlines.

The creation of the Indian-American did not come as an immediate result of "winning the West." It began in 1871 when Congress decreed that no longer were Indian tribes to be treated as independent powers, but rather the U.S. Government would manage tribal affairs without tribal consent. It continued by virtue of the Dawes Act of

Left:
WAGONS TO YUMA. 1983. Oil on canvas, 26x34 in. Collection Mr. Craig Singer. "When I was working on art for 'The Blue and the Gray,' I met the star of the miniseries, Stacey Keach. When I told him I wanted to paint his likeness, he said he would be honored. Here Stacey can be seen as a scout."

Right:
WHEN YOU CAN'T HIDE TRACKS. 1982. Oil on canvas, 22x30 in. Collection Mr. Robert R. Lockwood III. "The Indian wrapped in his Hudson Bay blanket knows there will be no escape from the troops, who will surely be led straight to him by the tracks he left in the snow."

Left:
CUSTER'S LAST STAND.
1986. Oil on canvas, 34x56 in.
Collection Mr. Robert E.
Mullane.

Top:
CHARGE! 1981. Opaque
watercolor, 15½x27¾ in.
Collection Mrs. Frank
Dickstein.

Above:
AND THEN ONE DAY THE
CIRCUS CAME TO TOWN.
1980. Oil on canvas, 30x40 in.
Collection "The Kiva," Beaver
Creek, Colorado.

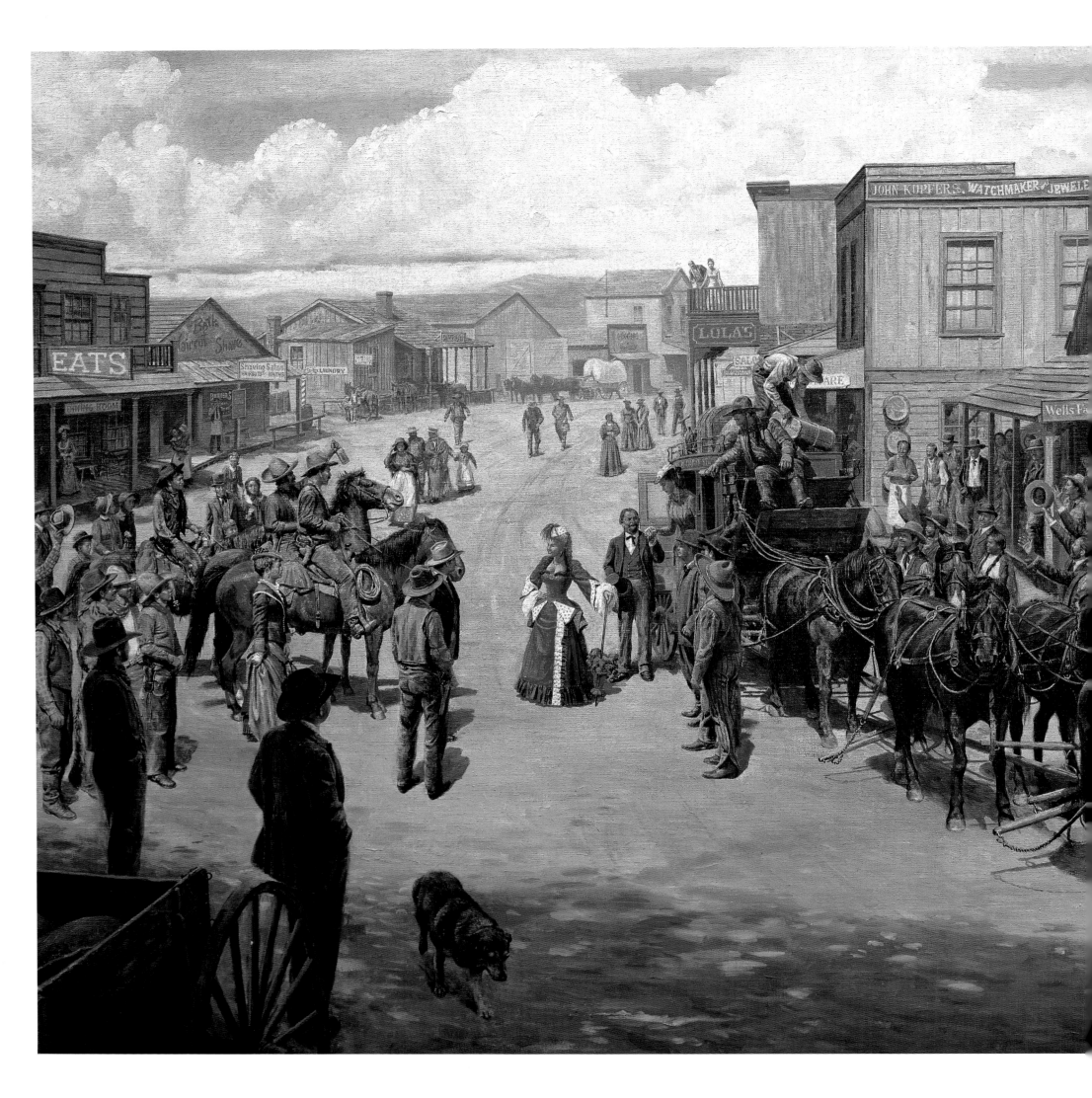

Above:
HOLIDAY CHEER. 1984.
Oil on canvas, 22x30 in.
Collection Mr. and Mrs. M.
Demenus.
"A lone cowboy on his way
into town passes a sodbuster
returning to his homestead
with supplies from town
and a Christmas tree from
the nearby mountainside."

Left:
NEW GIRLS IN TOWN.
1983. Oil on canvas, 30x40
in. Collection Mr. Craig
Singer.

1887—in effect until 1934—which allotted land to individual Indians rather than to tribes and opened all "surplus" lands to white settlers. If full assimilation—the desire of the reformist Indian Rights Association which had sponsored the act—had been the result, the loss of over sixty percent of Indian holdings might be overlooked. That was not the case. Granted full citizenship in 1924, and thus incorporated into the body politic, the Indian was rarely integrated into the social or economic fabric except at the lowest levels.

Above:
AMONGST THE SACRED ELDERBERRY. 1977. Oil on canvas, 26x20 in. Collection Hammer Galleries, New York.
"The Maidu used the elderberry wood to make split wood rattles."

Left:
OSOBAKI AND BUTU, SHAGGY HAIR AND FEATHER OF THE MAIDU. 1977. Oil on canvas, 26x20 in. Collection Mr. Harry Glass.
"The granddaughter and great-granddaughter of Marie Potts posed for this painting."

MARIE POTTS, CHENKUTPEM OF THE MAIDU. 1978. Oil on canvas, 16x13 in. Collection Mrs. Rhoda Gayle.
"I had the privilege of meeting Marie Potts and her family shortly before she died. Although she was not well at the time, she unhesitatingly posed for me. She was a truly remarkable woman."

Page 146:
STILL BEING USED. 1983. Oil on canvas, 16x20 in. Collection Mr. Charles Gates.
"This old chuck wagon is a fixture, almost a symbol, of the A Bar A Ranch. This painting is rather unusual for me, one of the few I have painted without figures."

The development of pan-Indian organizations such as the National Congress for American Indians, founded in the 1940s, opened a new era in Indian history. Once again the Indian took charge, resisting the government paternalism which had determined his plight since the end of hostilities. Working for the betterment of a race, rather than of independent tribes, such associations have had considerable effect. Gradually, the government has accepted self-determination as the proper goal of Indian policy. Marie Potts, is but one of the many individuals to be admired for her long and effective advocacy of the Indian cause. Member of the Maidu tribe, book author, and editor of an Indian newspaper in Sacramento, California, Mrs. Potts, or "One with Sharp Eyes"—her Indian name—died in 1977 at the age of eighty-two.

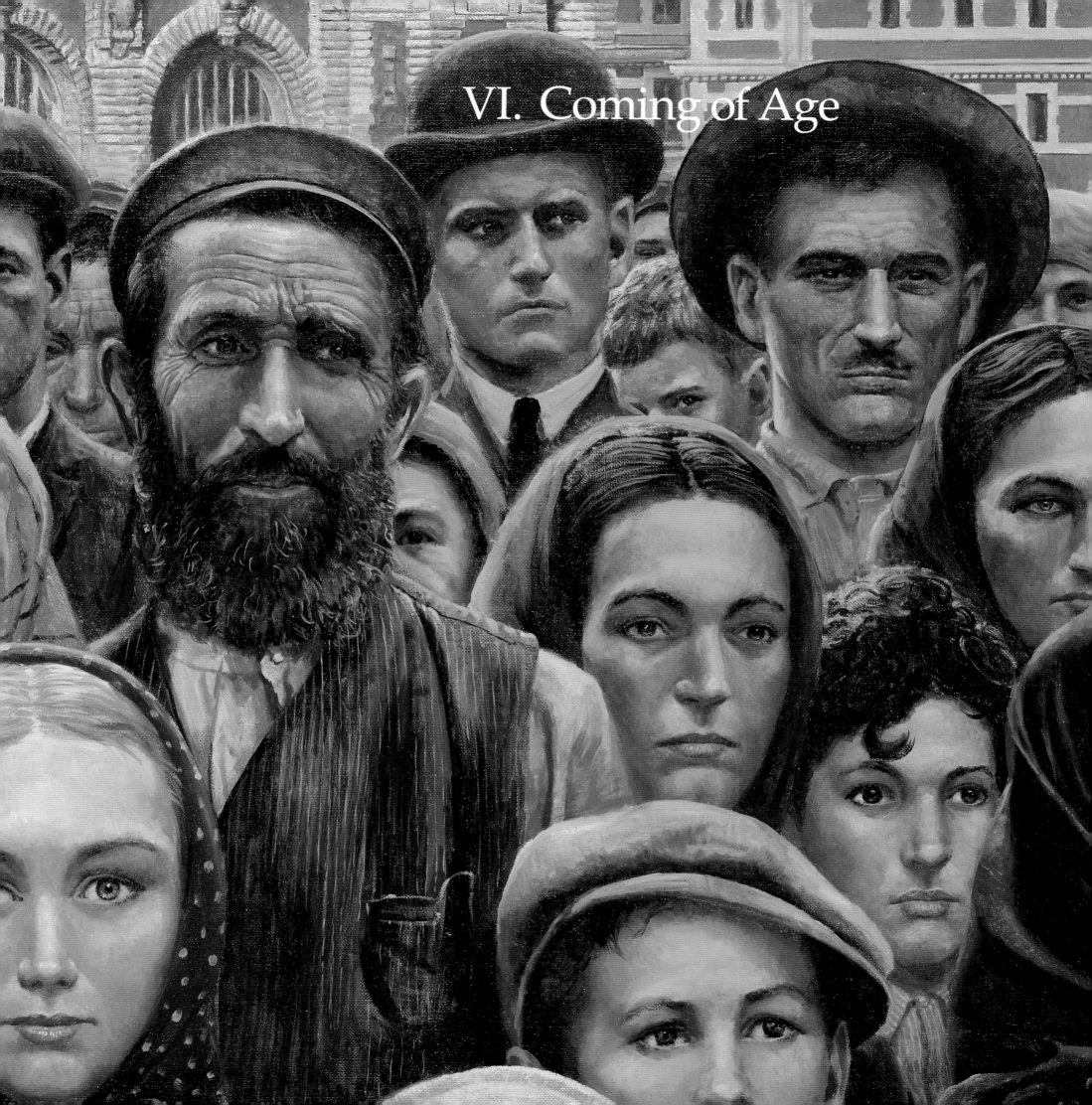

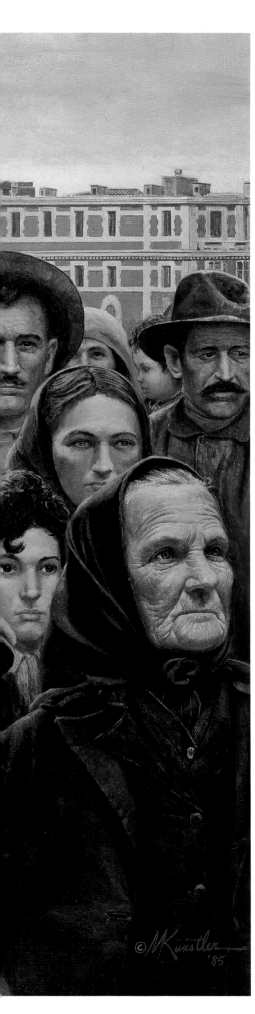

What does the phrase mean? Politically, America came of age with the Declaration of Independence and the Constitution: in the realm of politics she is, in many respects, the oldest and most sophisticated nation on the globe. Geographically, she came of age with the acquisition of all territory west to the Pacific and with the so-called "passing of the frontier," formally announced in 1890. Sociologically, she came of age in 1886, when, for the first time, the "new" emigration from southern and eastern Europe outstripped the "old" emigration from western and northern. Intellectually, she came of age with Ralph Waldo Emerson's "Address on the American Scholar" of 1837. Scientifically, she may claim to have come of age in 1907 when the first American scientist, Albert Michaelson, won the Nobel Prize in physics. And economically, Andrew Carnegie announced her maturity in the opening line of his *Triumphant Democracy* of 1886—"The old nations of the earth creep on at a snail's pace; the Republic thunders past with the rush of the Express"—but the Industrial Revolution can be dated from the 1790s when Eli Whitney invented the cotton gin and, a few years later, inaugurated the manufacture of guns on the principle of interchangeable parts.

Far more dramatic than these was the emergence of the United States as a world power in the 1890s. That can be dated, perhaps overdramatically, from the sinking of the battleship *Maine* in Havana harbor on February 15, 1898. The disaster—the cause of which has never been explained— led to a war to free Cuba from Spanish rule, and that war, in turn, brought about the annexation of Puerto Rico, the Philippines, and Hawaii. Thus, at one stroke, the United States, which ever since the Monroe Doctrine had rejected European intervention in the Americas and American intervention in the Old World, embraced the role of a world power. Leadership in that new role was eagerly embraced by President Theodore Roosevelt, who "took" Panama, arbitrated the Russo-Japanese War, built a giant navy and sent it around the world to display American prowess, and sat in on several European diplomatic conferences. After all this, "isolation" fought a rear-guard action and lost.

Page 147:
ELLIS ISLAND (Detail).

ELLIS ISLAND. 1985. Oil on canvas, 36x48 in. Collection Mr. and Mrs. Hans Reinecker. "This proved to be the most popular painting in my 1985 show at Hammer Galleries in New York."

OKLAHOMA LAND RUSH,
APRIL 22, 1889. 1988. Oil on
canvas, 22x50 in. Collection
John Gammill Company,
Oklahoma City, Oklahoma.

In the era of rapid industrialization and business monopoly that came after the Civil War, everything seemed to conspire against the organization of labor. A massive flow of immigration provided sources of cheap labor and of strike-breakers; rapid mechanization threw thousands of workers out of jobs without any provision for relief; giant corporations arose with almost limitless resources; conservative judicial interpretations paralyzed the use by labor of many of its most effective weapons such as the strike, the boycott, and picketing; the legal fiction of "liberty of contract" assumed that the individual worker was legally the equal of the corporation, and had the same right to make his own contracts; and the new doctrine of Social Darwinism applied to industrial society the principle of "survival of the fittest."

No wonder much of industrial history took on the character of open warfare. Thus, the violence of the Molly Maguires in the Pennsylvania coal mines, the great railroad strikes of 1877, the Haymarket "riot" of 1886, the Pullman strike of 1892—which jailed Eugene Debs and converted him

150

to socialism. None of these was more dramatic than the terrible strike of steel workers at Homestead, Pennsylvania, against the Carnegie Steel Company. Here Mr. Künstler depicts the culmination of that struggle—a pitched battle between infuriated strikers and Pinkerton detectives imported to end the strike. The strikers won the battle but lost the campaign when state militia moved in to "restore order." Such a "victory" enabled the steel industry to continue the twelve-hour day and the eighty-four-hour week until the steel strike of 1919.

Immigration is the great and pervasive theme of American history. All "Americans," except for the native Indians, were "newcomers." All—the English, Dutch, Spanish, Swedish, French, Scots, and Germans in the seventeenth and eighteenth centuries; the Danes, Norwegians, Finns, Italians, Irish, Poles, Greeks, Mexicans, Cubans, Asians, and Puerto Ricans in the nineteenth and twentieth centuries; the Africans at all times—nationalities from every continent uprooted themselves (or as in the case of the Africans were forcibly uprooted) from their familiar surroundings and folkways. All had to adjust to new environments, new institutions, and a new language. We shall never know how many immigrants sought the "Promised Land," or were brought here: the official total for the years since 1920 is a bit over fifty million; the total for three and a half centuries must be twice that.

From the founding of the nation until 1917 (after that time, quota restrictions were imposed by "old" Americans who feared that newcomers would somehow dilute the sacrosanct blood of an earlier race) the United States welcomed all newcomers and invited them to join its social, and eventually, its political community. Though not quite the melting pot the Jewish playright, Israel Zangwell, named it, America during those years did indeed prove to be a Promised Land to many. Every child in Scotland, so Andrew Carnegie assures us, knew that in America:

A man is a man if he's willing to toil
And the humblest may gather the fruit of the soil.
Their children are blessings, and he who has most
Has aid for his fortune and riches to boast.
There the young may exult and the aged may rest
Away far away, to the land of the West.

Top:
THE HOMESTEAD STEEL STRIKE. 1957. Opaque watercolor, blue and black, 16x33½ in. Collection Mr. and Mrs. B. Nichamoff.

Above:
FIRST PLEDGE OF ALLEGIANCE. 1977. Oil on board, 16x19³⁄₁₆ in. Collection Mr. Homer Noble.
"For this painting I used neighbors' children as models; I have since had the pleasure of seeing them grow up."

During most of the nineteenth century, immigrants were "processed" at Castle Garden in lower Manhattan, and, after 1892, at Ellis Island in the New York City harbor. Ellis Island remains associated in the American imagination with the gates to the Promised Land. This association was celebrated in a score of novels and autobiographies written by immigrants, and is indelibly inscribed in the memories of millions of American families. That association was powerfully reenforced by the location, on nearby Bedloe's Island, of what has claim to be the most famous statue in history—the Statue of Liberty. This colossal monument, the gift of the French people on the one-hundredth anniversary of American independence, was the work of the illustrious French sculptor Frederic Bartholdi and the American architect Richard Morris Hunt. The competition for the inscription was, appropriately enough, won by an American-born girl of Russian-Jewish parents, Emma Lazarus:

Not like the brazen giant of Greek fame,
With conquering limbs astride from land to land;
Here at our sea-washed sunset gates shall stand
A mighty woman with a torch, whose flame
Is the imprisoned lightning, and her name
Mother of Exiles. From her beacon-hand
Glows world-wide welcome; her mild eyes command
The air-bridged harbor that twin cities frame.
"Keep, ancient lands, your storied pomp," cries she
With silent lips. "Give me your tired, your poor,
Your huddled masses yearning to breathe free,
The wretched refuse of your teeming shore.
Send these, the homeless, tempest-tost to me,
I lift my lamp beside the golden door!"

FIRST VIEW OF THE LADY. 1986. Oil on canvas, 36x48 in. Collection Mr. and Mrs. Hans Reinecker.

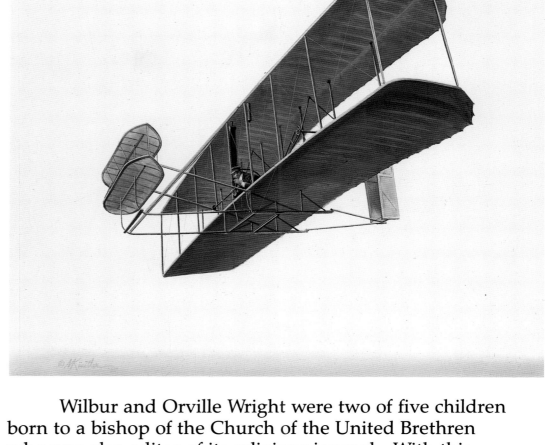

Wilbur and Orville Wright were two of five children
born to a bishop of the Church of the United Brethren
who was also editor of its religious journal. With this
background, it might have been expected that they would
pursue clerical or academic careers. Instead, fascinated from
boyhood by mechanical toys, gadgets, and machinery, they
followed the paths of science and invention. Scarcely out of
school, they built their own printing press, on which they
printed their own newspaper. Tiring of this, they turned to
a new fad—bicycles—which they built and sold with considerable success. By 1890, balloons, which had served the
Union Army well in the Civil War, caught their attention.

Serious experiments in aviation began in the early
1890s when they built a model biplane with a five-foot
wingspread. A few years later they moved to Kitty Hawk,
on Albermarle Sound, North Carolina, where they set up
what was perhaps the first aviation laboratory in the country. After hundreds of experiments with glider planes in a
specially built wind tunnel, they managed to build a plane,
powered by a twelve-horsepower motor, but one which had
to be launched by a catapult, and, to make matters worse,
the pilot had to lie on his stomach to operate. Three years
later, Orville was able to launch a gasoline-powered plane; it
flew some two hundred feet and stayed aloft a full minute.
On December 17 of that same year, Wilbur managed to stay
aloft for a full minute and fly over eight hundred feet: the
Age of Aviation had arrived.

In the mid-1890s, Theodore Roosevelt, scion of a distinguished Knickerbocker family, was a young man on the rise; but he had not yet decided whether he would be a great historian, a great soldier, or a great statesman. As it turned out, he did pretty well in all three capacities.

Because young Roosevelt was ardent for good government, President Harrison made him a civil service commissioner, which gave him the opportunity both to live in Washington and to become intimate with writers and statesmen. Because he had friends at court, as it were, McKinley made him Assistant Secretary of the Navy. When the sinking of the battleship *Maine* in Cuban waters made war almost inevitable, Roosevelt—with characteristic impetuosity—cabled Admiral Dewey to make sure the Spanish fleet did not leave Asiatic waters, and to "prepare for offensive operations in the Philippines." Then, impatient with a sedentary job, he teamed up with Colonel Leonard Wood to raise a special regiment of "Rough Riders"—a term he coined—to be drawn from cattlemen, miners, big game hunters, and others, for service in the coming war. The regiment was duly organized; Wood was appointed colonel and Roosevelt, lieutenant-colonel: neither had any experience in actual combat. With the declaration of war, they were off to Tampa for desultory training, and in mid-June, *sans* horses, they embarked for Santiago, Cuba, in whose spacious harbor the Spanish fleet had assembled; the Spanish army had dug in atop the ridge of San Juan Hill.

The battle came on July 1, 1898. In the face of heavy fire the Americans managed to gain the heights and disperse the Spanish defenses. Confronted by disaster the Spanish fleet took to sea, where it was met by devastating fire from five battleships and two cruisers. The Spanish fleet was totally

THE ROUGH RIDERS. 1984. Oil on canvas, 24x32 in. Collection National Guard Bureau, Pentagon. "I was absolutely delighted when I received this commission from the Pentagon. Sagamore Hill National Historic Site, the former home of Teddy Roosevelt, is less than a mile from my house, and I have lived in the Oyster Bay area ('Teddy Roosevelt country') for more than twenty years. Knowing many members of the Roosevelt family gave this painting an even more special meaning for me."

Sketch:
ROUGH RIDERS.

destroyed at the cost of only one man in the American flotilla. That, in effect, ended the Spanish-American War.

Thus opened a new chapter in the history of the United States, with the temporary acquisition of Cuba and the long-term acquisition of Puerto Rico, the Philippines, Guam and Hawaii. It opened a new chapter, too, for Roosevelt. Hastening home, he soon produced one of his most popular books, *The Rough Riders.* The book was "reviewed" by the most widely read of American humorists, Finley Peter Dunne, whose Mr. Dooley said:

I haven't time f'r to tell ye the wurruck Tiddy did in arhimn an' equippin himself, how he fed himself, how he steadied himself in battles and encouraged himself with a few well-chosen wurruds whin th' sky was darkest. But if I was him I'd call the book "Alone in Cubia."

The "review," far from harming T.R., merely added to his popularity. Roosevelt went home to become Governor of New York and then, in 1900, to be chosen for the vice-presidency. When, in September of 1901, President McKinley was assassinated by a crazed office-seeker, the Republican boss, Mark Hanna, exclaimed "Now that damned cowboy is President of the United States!"

When, in 1953, Edmund Hillary was asked why he had been willing to risk his life climbing to the top of Mt. Everest, he replied quite simply, "because it was there." That has been the *cri de coeur* of explorers and adventurers, of scientists and inventors, from the beginning of history. The passion to "conquer" the North Pole—and after that the South—emerged in the 1880s when, for the first time, it seemed possible of realization. As early as 1886, young Robert Edwin Peary, of the United States Coast and Geodetic Survey, visited Greenland and conceived the idea of reaching the North Pole. Others, too, were inspired by that ambition—none more distinguished than the Norwegian Frithjov Nansen, who had crossed Greenland in 1889 and, in 1893, launched the first major polar expedition.

That same year, and each year thereafter, Peary penetrated Greenland even farther north toward the pole. In 1897 he won the backing of the British magnate Lord Northcliffe, and in 1905 he returned to the challenge in his specially constructed ship, the *Roosevelt:* that venture had to be abandoned some two hundred miles from the pole. Finally, in the winter of 1908–9, with four Eskimos and one black man, Matthew Henson, Peary fought his way over the ice and on April 6, 1909, was able to raise the United States flag at the North Pole. His triumph was marred by the claim of Dr. Frederick Cook that he had actually reached the pole a year earlier. Eventually, however, Peary's claim to discovery was conceded. Acclaimed in two continents, he was promoted to rear admiral of the navy and heaped with honors. "To say that my motives were entirely unselfish," he later confessed, "would be incorrect, but I can say that the desire to win honorable and lasting reputation went hand in hand with the desire to add to the sum total of human knowledge."

Perhaps the simplest definition of democracy is that which Lincoln gave in his Gettysburg Address: "Government of the people, by the people, for the people." Though, when in 1789 Washington gave his Inaugural Address, he spoke to what was incomparably the most democratic society in the world, actual democracy in terms of majority rule had made very little progress. A good many white males, all blacks, and all women were excluded.

Efforts to change all that go back to the anti-slavery

THE FLAG REACHES THE NORTH POLE. 1977. Oil on board, 17¼x19¼ in. Collection Mr. Homer Noble. "Peary brought this silk flag, handmade by his wife, on each of his many expeditions in search of the North Pole. On every unsuccessful attempt, he cut a small square from the flag, secreted it in a jar, and buried it at the northernmost point. Finally, on his sixth try, he reached his goal; there he cut a three-inch diagonal swath from the flag. The white patches used to replace the missing pieces are visible in this picture."

crusade of William Lloyd Garrison's day, and particularly to 1840 when two intrepid young women, Lucretia Mott and Elisabeth Cady Stanton, went to London to participate in a World Anti-Slavery Convention only to find that they were not allowed to speak or even to sit in the convention itself, but were relegated to the gallery. They returned to America determined to free not only blacks from slavery, but women from semi-slavery.

Their first step in that direction came in 1848 when they organized the famous Seneca Falls, New York, convention, which in the language of the Declaration of Independence arraigned the tyranny of men over women, and called for "immediate admission to all the rights and privileges which belong to them as citizens of the United States."

That immediate recognition was a long time coming. Finally, in 1869, the Territory of Wyoming led the way by granting women suffrage; gradually, other states followed, mostly those in the West. By the time of the First World War, thirteen states had adopted women's suffrage. Clearly the demand for equality could no longer be denied: women served alongside men as nurses during the war and, even more importantly, took over many jobs—in both industry and the office—left untended when the men went to war. By 1917, New York joined the roster of states embracing women's suffrage, and victory was in sight.

Confronting a reluctant Congress, women followed the example set by the suffragettes of England. They paraded, agitated, demonstrated, went on hunger strikes, and chained themselves to the White House fences. Belatedly—and even reluctantly—President Wilson came out on their side "as a war measure," and in the summer of 1919 Congress passed the Nineteenth Amendment to the Constitution, which stated that "the right of citizens of the United States to vote shall not be denied by the United States, or by any State on account of sex."

Thereafter, notwithstanding implacable hostility in most of the southern states, the amendment was ratified by three-fourths of the states in record time; on August 18, 1920, the Nineteenth Amendment became part of the Constitution.

SUFFRAGETTES. 1987. Oil on canvas, 19x25 in. Collection of the artist.

The philosophies of Jefferson's generation, committed as they were to the notion that the farmer was the favored child of God, were passionately devoted to the advancement of farming through science. The average American farmer, however, had little interest in what science might contribute. As one book on farming, published in 1860, put it, "scientific agriculture stands today with phrenology and biology and magnetism. No farmer ever yet received any benefit from any analysis of the soil and none ever will." Two years later Congress, in the Morrill Act, created state universities devoted primarily to agriculture and engineering sciences; and in 1887, the Hatch Act set up agricultural experiment stations in every state of the Union.

In the 1840s, the western frontier, which had advanced progressively for two centuries, reached the edge of the Great Plains. Then instead of continuing its progressive advance, it leaped fifteen hundred miles to Oregon and California. For almost forty years the intervening land—some of the richest in the world—was almost uninhabited except by Indians, by Mormons driven from Illinois and Missouri, and by miners and cattlemen. Not until the late 1870s did farmers resume their traditional westward migration.

The explanation of this phenomenon is simple enough. Almost from the beginning of American map-making, the vast region from Arizona to the Dakotas had been dubbed the "Great American Desert." To eastern eyes it looked treeless; it was almost without navigable rivers; its annual rainfall was below twenty inches a year. It was a land where the American farmer could no longer rely on those tools and methods of farming he had brought with him from Europe, tools and methods to which he had been accustomed for two hundred years. The attempts of settlers to farm this arid land resulted at first in economic and social ruin; this continued until new methods such as dry farming and the windmill were developed for getting water, and new techniques of fencing and ploughing and reaping and threshing were introduced—until, in short, "a plainscraft took the place of woodscraft." That revolution came in the 1870s and gathered momentum all through the next half century with the elimination of the Indian and the buffalo, the construction of railroads and of grain elevators, the introduction of barbed wire fencing and of new varieties of disease-resistant wheat and corn, and the use of farm

THE OVERSHOT STACKER. 1975. Oil on canvas, 26x40 in. Collection Hesston Corp. "My old friend Vaden Stroud acted as my expert consultant for all my farm paintings, and posed for most of the figures in this painting."

machinery adapted to the requirements of farms that stretched over thousands of acres.

Mechanization of agriculture did not really begin until the 1830s and 40s, when Cyrus McCormick was experimenting with a reaper, George Westinghouse with a thresher, and John Deere with a chilled plough. Farm machinery remained relatively unimportant until the Civil War, when it replaced the labor of a million young men then in the armies, and enabled the United States to export vast quantities of grain to Britain and Europe. After that war came countless new inventions to revolutionize farming. There were no less than twelve thousand patents for ploughs given before 1900. Soon almost every operation from preparing the ground to harvesting the product was transformed by machinery. The Oliver chilled plough was perfected in 1877; in 1878 came the Appleby twine binder and the steam threshing machine. Within twenty years every large farm was using combines, which reaped, threshed, gleaned, and bagged the grain in a single operation.

During the same years the corn planter, corn binder, cornhusker, and corn sheller, the manure spreader, the potato planter, the mechanical hay drier, the cream separator, and innumerable other machines completely transformed

Left:
HARVESTING WHEAT. 1974. Oil on canvas, 30x40 in. Collection Hesston Corp. "Commissioned by Don Blair of Santa Fe's Blair Galleries, I traveled in Kansas and Nebraska for several weeks during the June harvest to learn all I could about wheat and the machinery used to gather it."

Right:
THRESHING WHEAT. 1974. Oil on canvas, 30x40 in. Collection Hesston Corp. "Vaden Stroud once complimented me on my farm paintings: 'For a New York City boy, you sure painted these pictures like the biggest expert there is!' Of course, as my 'expert,' he checked all the details along the way."

the ancient practices of farming. In the twentieth century came the application of steam, gasoline and electricity to the farm. The result of this was predictable, but nonetheless spectacular. While the total number of farms in the country declined steadily from almost 6 million in 1900 to less than half that number in 1970, the production of wheat increased from less than 500 million to over 2 billion bushels and of corn from less than 2 billion to over 6 billion bushels. Farming as a way of life gave way to farming as a business.

One of the most reactionary of American industrialists was also, despite himself, one of the most revolutionary. The conservatism was personal and emotional, the radicalism impersonal and scientific. In his economic philosophy he belonged firmly in the nineteenth century; his mechanical genius made him a harbinger of the twentieth. It was Henry Ford's contribution to the creation of an automobile economy and culture that makes him one of the "makers and shakers" of the world we live in. If he did not "invent" the automobile—credit for that belongs to French and German mechanics—he was a seminal figure in making it the most essential, and the most universal, machine in modern life; and he came, quite rightly, to symbolize the automobile as Carnegie symbolized steel and Rockefeller oil.

A self-trained mechanical genius, he built his first automobile in 1896 and created the Ford Motor Company in 1903; by 1908 he had introduced the moving assembly line—an idea as revolutionary as Eli Whitney's principle of interchangeable parts. That same year he launched the ever-famous Model T (the "flivver"). The assembly line made possible not only mass production, but a reduction in price (by 1916) to $360, thus changing the "car" from a Richman's luxury to Everyman's necessity.

The automobile created, and became the center of, a whole new economy—a kind of industrial-transportation-financial complex. Increasingly the national economy came to depend on the prosperity of this complex, which embraced steel, cement, glass, rubber, machine tools, and, above all, oil. Psychologically it conjured up what might be called an "automobile civilization." How right Aldous Huxley was to have the inhabitants of his Brave New World worship "Our Ford."

**STROUD FARM. 1976.
Oil on board, 24¾x32¼ in.
Collection Mr. Roy
Lawrence.**
"This painting was conceived as a tribute to Vaden Stroud. It depicts the Stroud Farm in Hutchinson, Kansas, the way it could have looked in late summer of 1917. The waterboy in the foreground is Vaden the way he might have looked back then."

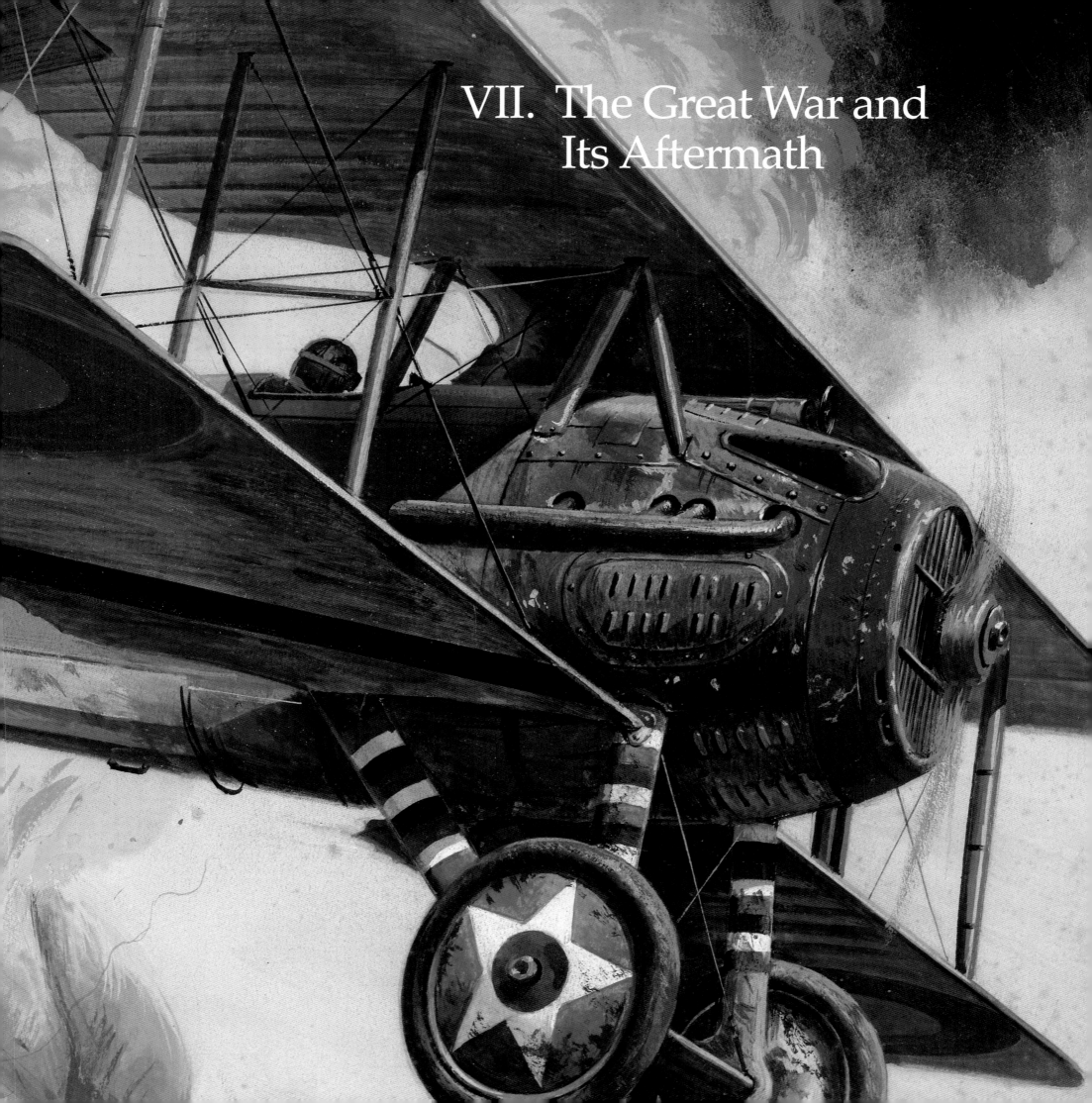

VII. The Great War and
Its Aftermath

VII. THE GREAT WAR AND ITS AFTERMATH

As late as the summer of 1916, President Wilson campaigned for the presidency on the slogan that he had "kept us out of war." Then the German U-boat campaign that winter, plus the declining military fortunes of the Allies, persuaded him the United States would have to come to the aid of the Allies in order to save both freedom and democracy. On April 6, 1917, Congress ratified this view. The nation was singularly unprepared for war, but for the most part shifted its industry to a war basis with remarkable speed and efficiency. The navy got in the thick of the fight almost at once; and the first American army contingents reached France in June of 1917, and could march down the Champs Elysées on Independence Day—allowing Colonel Stanton to pronounce the historic words, "LaFayette, we are here."

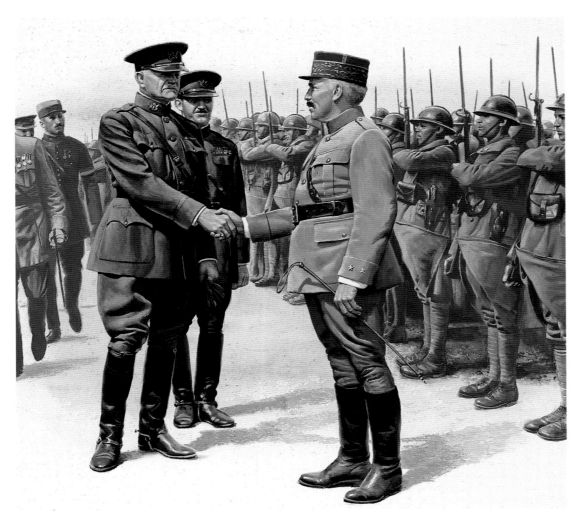

Page 171:
**RICK NAILS A DRACHEN
(Detail):**

**GENERAL PERSHING
ARRIVES IN FRANCE.**
1985. Opaque watercolor,
12x14 in. Collection
Fleetwood, Division of
Unicover Corp., Cheyenne,
Wyoming.

Right:
RICK NAILS A DRACHEN.
1964. Opaque watercolor,
19x23 in. Collection Col.
and Mrs. Stanley Ulanoff.
"I found an actual 'Spad' in
flying condition at the
Rhinebeck Aerodrome in
upstate New York to use as
a model for this painting of
Eddie Rickenbacker shooting
down a German balloon."

SILVER GHOST, AUTUMN LEAVES. 1976. Oil on board, 24x31 in. Collection Mr. Roy Lawrence. "The car and the mansion I found on Long Island, the model for the woman was Debbi, and I posed for the driver. It was fun to do—and none of the models charged for the job!"

The military's aviation program was, by contrast, a disaster: no American-built plane reached France in time to engage in combat. Meantime, eager young Americans had enlisted in the LaFayette Esquadrille, and, with United States entry into the war, a newly recruited American air force flew French and British planes. Among the American flyers who distinguished themselves, none caught the popular imagination more than "Eddie" Rickenbacker, who, as pilot with the 94th Aero Pursuit Squadron (the first U. S. squadron to go into action), shot down a total of twenty-six enemy planes. After the war, Rickenbacker had a long and successful career in commercial aviation and, with the coming of World War II, enlisted his talents once again in building up an American air force.

Mr. Künstler has pictured Rickenbacker shooting down a German balloon. His own plane bears the "hat-in-the-ring" insignia adopted—and still retained—by the 94th Squadron. Uncle Sam's stovepipe hat was tossed into the ring, inviting the enemy to battle.

"Jazz," applied to music, came out of late nineteenth-century New Orleans; it was the gifted F. Scott Fitzgerald who in his *Tales of the Jazz Age* (1922) first used it as the name of an era, and who was its most skillful literary historian. He was the chronicler of the very rich, who preferred to live in Paris, or the Rivera, or, at the very least, on the North Shore of Long Island; and of the near-rich, who yearned to be very. He wrote of the great Prosperity and the great Bust of the twenties; of that Hollywood whose striking characteristic was that "when you got through the artificial tinsel, you came to the real tinsel." His stories and novels recreated the other side of the society whose faithful historian was the Sinclair Lewis of *Main Street* and *Babbitt*.

Mr. Künstler's painting might be an illustration for *The Great Gatsby*, that desperate figure, who, in a sense, symbolized the Jazz Age: the Great Jay Gatsby, whose wealth was as obscure as his social credentials. His life mirrors the economic and social fantasies of the decade. Here, in a curious blend of fancy and achievement is a dream life: the phony Oxford education, the phony cosmopolitanism, the real jewels that, nevertheless, managed to be artificial, the great estate on Long Island with its Marie Antoinette music room where nobody played. Here, too, were the dream cars: "rich cream in color, bright with nickel, swollen here and there in their monstrous length with triumphant hat boxes and supper boxes, and terraces with a labyrinth of windshields that mirrored a dozen suns."

Gatsby yearned for the realization of his illusion but—like the decade—was unable to delude even himself. As effectively as Thorstein Veblen, Fitzgerald laid bare the pathology of the leisure classes and of their big money.

Sketch:
THE GAME.

Right:
THE GAME. 1982. Oil on canvas, 25⅛x32 in. Collection Mr. J. Sirulnick. "Here is a tailgate party at a Yale-Harvard game — vintage 1928. Since this is during Prohibition, that sure isn't coffee in the cups the people are holding! The picnic set in the foreground was particularly hard to come by — a friend of mine, an antique car buff, owns it."

Time itself seems to go faster in America than in the Old World, and antiquity is measured in decades rather than in centuries. Mr. Künstler has evoked here a past of only half a century, but his picture has the quality and the mood of a Currier and Ives print or, perhaps, of the genre paintings of a George Caleb Bingham, a Sidney Mount, an Eastman Johnson, who recorded so faithfully the lives of simple people in mid-nineteenth-century America. Yet the scene here is modern enough to be, if not familiar, at least recognizable, and the juxtaposition of the horse-drawn wagon, the "depot hack," with its Model T engine and its specially fabricated body, and the railroad train seems natural enough. The horse and wagon are pretty much a thing of the past, but the station wagon is very much with us, and if railroad trains are becoming increasingly rare in small towns, Amtrak is making a valiant effort to restore them. The mood of nostalgia which broods over this *Holiday Homecoming* is increasingly common in American art; it suffuses much of the work of Grant Wood and John Stuart Curry and even John Sloan and Maurice Prendergast.

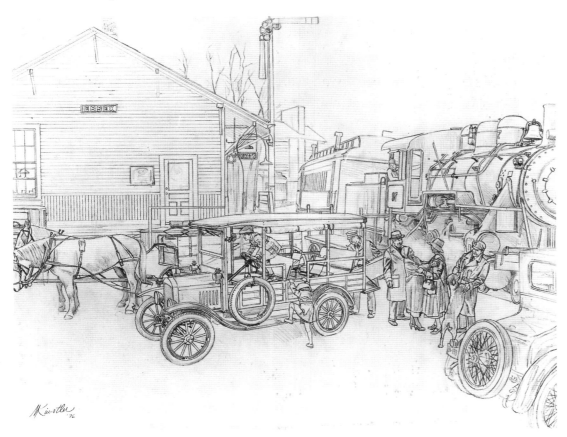

Sketch:
HOLIDAY HOMECOMING.

Right:
HOLIDAY HOMECOMING.
1976. Oil on board, 26x34 in. Collection Mr. Donald L. Criqui.
"For this painting I combined the train and station from Essex, Connecticut, a horse and wagon from Old Bethpage Village, and cars from elsewhere on Long Island. Again my wife posed for the young woman, but this time my nephew is the one at the steering wheel."

THE SPIRIT OF ST. LOUIS.
1985. Opaque watercolor,
8x9½ in. Collection Mr. E.
Davidson.
"It is wonderful for an artist
to have resources like the
Smithsonian Institution.
Instead of hunting down old
photographs on which to
base my likeness, I was able
to go to Washington to see
the real plane, look at it
from every angle, and then
paint it from the one I felt
worked the best."

A nation's choice of heroes tells a great deal about its character. In the class societies of the Old World, those who ruled, or who commanded, were almost automatically called "great"—thus Frederick the Great, Catherine the Great or Louis XIV "the Sun King", and thus the uncritical adulation of a Marlborough, a Nelson, or a Napoleon. In America those who are esteemed great have rarely been military heroes: Washington is remembered as the Father of his Country; Lincoln as the Great Emanicipator; and of Civil War heroes it is Robert E. Lee rather than U. S. Grant, who defeated him, who is a national hero.

In our own time it is Charles Lindbergh who was exalted to the position of greatness. While the history of aviation has counted many heroes, it is Lindbergh alone who has achieved both universal and lasting fame—Lindbergh who, flying his little *Spirit of St. Louis*, made the first solo nonstop flight across the Atlantic on May 20–21, 1927, and thus became a living symbol of the conquest of the skies.

No wonder that Lindbergh, all but mobbed on his arrival in Paris, found himself a national hero on his return to the United States; hero to a complacent people who, with Calvin Coolidge as their respectable but dull Head of State, longed for heroics. A personable young man, Lindbergh bore his fame with modesty and avoided rather than sought publicity and celebrity. His interest in aviation was scientific, not adventurous or commercial. With the approach of World War II, he was appointed colonel and then brigadier general in the air force, and served on the board of West Point and the Air Force Academy and worked effectively for the conservation of natural resources. As his fame grew, so too did his passion for privacy. As he withdrew into seclusion, he became even more a figure of legend.

The stock market crash of October 1929 ushered in the greatest domestic crisis since the attack upon Fort Sumter. It came with an abruptness unprecedented in our economic past; it cut deeper and spread wider than any previous crisis of its kind, and it lasted longer. In the plunge, too, from prosperity to widespread ruin it was more dramatic than anything in our earlier history, and with a kind of poetic justice it came just a year after the newly elected President Hoover had announced that "the choice before the people [was] the American system of rugged individualism

**THE GREAT DEPRESSION.
c. 1955. Gouache, 17x25 in.
Collection of the artist.
"The earliest painting in the
book, this was painted as a
magazine illustration.
Although I would do it
much differently today, I
still like the composition
and the feeling of this
work."**

or the European philosophy of 'paternalism and socialism.' "

Within a few months the stock market crash pre-cipitated a crisis in every segment of the American econ-omy. Thousands of businesses were plunged into bankruptcy. Over five thousand banks closed their doors to frantic depositors, unemployment passed the five, then the ten million mark; foreign trade declined from nine to three billion dollars; and farmers faced catastrophe as wheat plunged from almost two dollars to thirty-six cents a bushel while cotton fell to less than five cents a pound. Con-fronted with all this, President Hoover and the Republican Senate clung stubbornly to "rugged individualism," while in city after city the workless were forced out of their homes and into makeshift packing-box shelters that quickly got the name of Hoovervilles.

The most notorious of all Hoovervilles was that constructed by the so-called Bonus Army. It was in June 1932, with a presidential election in the offing, that an "army" of desperate veterans of the war, pleading in vain for immediate payment of the bonus that Congress had voted them, took matters into their own hands and marched on Washington where they camped just below the Capitol. By mid-summer there were 17,000 of them, many with wives and children, attempting in vain to excite presidential sympathy and support. Outraged by what he thought was not only illegal action but a desecration of the Capitol, Hoover ordered them to go home. Most obeyed, but a stubborn remnant defied the order and held their ground. On July 28, with characteristic ineptitude, Hoover ordered the National Guard under General Douglas MacArthur to drive out the pitiful veterans and their families and set fire to their ramshackle shelters and belongings. It was the one achievement of Hoover's administration that to this day lingers in the public mind. That fall he lost the presidency to Franklin Roosevelt by over seven million votes.

THE BONUS ARMY
MARCHES. c. 1958.
Pencil drawing, 12x17 in.
Collection of the artist.

Right:
THE BATTLE OF
ANACOSTIA FLATS.
c. 1958. Mixed media,
14x22 in. Collection of
the artist.
"A very complex picture,
this magazine assignment
had to be done in three
days. I used a very
different technique of line
and wash, spending most
of my time to draw it up."

182

Franklin Delano Roosevelt came to the presidency at the depth of the greatest depression in American history—a crisis which seemed to threaten the very foundations of the Republic. Could the situation be saved: could the descent into poverty and misery be reversed?

A two-term governor of New York, Roosevelt was not unknown to the American people; but few of those who rejoiced in the political repudiation of the old order were prepared for the boldness, the courage, the political mastery, and the creativity he displayed. "We have nothing to fear but fear itself," he said in his inaugural address; and he promptly asked Congress to give him "broad executive power such as would be given me if we were invaded by a foreign power." Congress granted his request, and Roosevelt responded with a program as bold and comprehensive as the one that Alexander Hamilton submitted to the first American Congress.

Within three months Roosevelt had pushed through an eager Congress a body of legislation designed to halt and reverse the Depression. It was, he said, not a revolution but a "New Deal" for the American people. One part of the New Deal was a program to relieve the desperate unemployment and poverty, both in the cities and on the farms. Another looked not just to immediate relief but to far-reaching reforms. By 1940 Roosevelt had pumped some twenty-five billion dollars into the economy, and by that time, far-reaching and fundamental reforms were already underway. These included a series of measures designed to save and restore the natural resources of the nation, to rescue the railroads, and to provide government support to both private and public housing and relief to the stricken cities across the land.

Reform was even bolder, for it looked to a reconstruction which might forever banish depression and poverty: thus the Tennessee Valley Authority, designed to be a model for regional control of electrical power, and prosperous regional economies; thus the conservation of natural resources by building a hundred-mile-wide belt of forests at the edge of the High Plains, and by constructing thousands of dams and bridges and waterways. All this restored not only the economy but the confidence of the people.

During his second term of office, with the support of all but two states, Congress enacted a national system of so-

F.D.R. 1985. Opaque watercolor, 8x6 in. Collection Mr. S. Lesnick.

Left:
THE HINDENBURG. 1975. Oil on illustration board, 28x24¾ in. Collection 20th Century-Fox Corp. "Commissioned by Fox to advertise the movie *The Hindenburg*, I first went to previews of the movie, then worked with movie stills, old photographs, and models of the zeppelin."

cial security and health care, a charter of liberties for labor, with the first national prohibition of child labor, and a national housing program. All this looked to the transformation of a highly individualistic corporate economy into one which took seriously those goals set forth in the Constitution itself: to establish justice and to provide for the general welfare.

The fulfillment of the promise of the New Deal was shattered by the outbreak of World War II. Elected to an unprecedented third term, Roosevelt devoted his energies to aiding the Allies as effectively as he could without actually entering into the war. Roosevelt persuaded the Congress to transfer fifty destroyers to Britain and, more importantly, to launch a vast program of "Lend-Lease" which provided supplies of all kinds essential to the safety of the Allied nations "whose survival was essential to the safety of the United States." More than any other action before Pearl Harbor, Lend-Lease made it possible for Great Britain and the Soviet Union to fight on.

In the aftermath of Pearl Harbor, Roosevelt joined in the greatest military feat in history: fighting and winning a two-ocean war. Roosevelt lived to know that victory was certain, but not to witness the final consummation of his hopes. His last words before his pen dropped from lifeless hands provide a fitting epitaph to his life: "The only limit to our realization of tomorrow will be our doubts of today. Let us move forward with strong and active faith."

VIII. World War II and
the Modern Era

The most titanic military conflict in history—with the fate of many old and famous nations hanging in the balance—reached what Winston Churchill called a "grand climacteric" with the Japanese attack upon our naval base at Pearl Harbor on the morning of December 7, 1941. It was a date, said President Franklin Roosevelt, "that shall live in infamy." For the American navy it was a catastrophe: 6 battleships, 2 naval auxiliaries, 3 destroyers, 149 planes and over 3,500 casualties; all at a cost to the Japanese of only 30 planes. That day, Japan wiped out General MacArthur's air force grounded at Manila and bombed Guam, Saipan, and Singapore.

It was the most costly defeat ever suffered by the United States, but, as it proved, it was for the Japanese the most costly victory. Their infamous attack violated one of the major principles of warfare: if you strike a king, strike to kill. The attack on Pearl Harbor knocked out the Pacific fleet, but it did not knock out the United States; rather it united the American people and fired its will to victory as nothing else could have done. Within six months of Pearl Harbor, a reconstructed and vastly enlarged American navy inflicted on the Japanese at Midway their first naval defeat, and one from which they never recovered. Within one year, the nation the Japanese had hoped to knock out launched successful offensives in two quarters of the globe—the Solomon Islands and North Africa—and both were crowned with victory.

Over in beleaguered London, Winston Churchill, the most farsighted statesman of his age, had seen this, and greeted Pearl Harbor with exultation. "So we had won after all," he later wrote. "England would live. Britain would live. The Commonwealth of Nations would live.... As for the Japanese, they would be ground to powder." And so they were—the Japanese and the Italians and the Germans, all who had underestimated American will and resourcefulness. Churchill's instinct and confidence were sound. "American blood flowed in my veins," he wrote. "I had studied the American Civil War, fought out to the last desperate inch. I went to bed and slept the sleep of the saved and the thankful."

Page 187:
SAY GOODBYE, DEAR, I'LL SEE YOU NEXT YEAR (Detail).

SAY GOODBYE, DEAR, I'LL SEE YOU NEXT YEAR. 1983. Oil on canvas, 24x32 in. Collection National Guard Bureau, Pentagon. "The members of Battery C, 2nd Battalion, 189 Field Artillery from Blackwell, Oklahoma, were called up for one year of training on September 23, 1940. Those who returned after the war wound up serving more than five years on battlefields all over the world. This is the way the scene might have looked on that early fall morning more than forty-five years ago."

For two years the Russians, fighting desperately for survival, had clamored, in vain, for a "second front"—an Anglo-American invasion of Europe from the west. In agreement with the Russians that such a front would be necessary for victory, both Roosevelt and Churchill knew full well how hazardous such an operation would be, how prodigious the efforts required to carry it to success. Unable to amass the forces to assure success before 1944, they concentrated, instead, on the reconquest of North Africa and the invasion of Italy, and on an aerial bombardment with the hope that it would destroy the German capacity for war. But never for a moment did they abandon the conviction that Germany could be defeated only by invading armies.

At the Teheran Conference, Churchill and Roosevelt promised Stalin that they would launch an invasion in May or June of 1944, and to this pledge they were faithful. After preparations, the most extensive in military history, the invasion was launched on "D-Day" (which meant, with deceptive simplicity, the "day") June 5–6, 1944. On the first night, three paratroop divisions were dropped behind the

Above:
THIS WE'LL DEFEND.
1976. Oil on canvas, 24x18 in. Collection Mrs. Deborah Künstler.
"This symbolic painting was done for the United States Army bicentennial as a limited edition print, as well as appearing on the cover of *Army* magazine."

Right:
PEARL HARBOR—A ZERO DOWN! 1960. Opaque watercolor, 13½x14¾ in. Collection Mrs. Janet Damon.
"Painted for a magazine cover illustration, as was much of the World War II art I did during the 1960s, this painting's main objectives were action and color."

Far right:
D-DAY. c. 1960. Mixed media, 18¾x16½ in. Collection Mr. William Cole.
"During the late 1950s I began to accumulate all kinds of props and costumes to help me with my work. I own all the guns, helmets, uniforms, etc. that are seen in this painting—everything, that is, but the landing craft!"

German lines; early the next morning, the Americans launched the great assault at Utah and Omaha beaches on a forty-mile strip along the Normandy coast, and the numerically superior British began the struggle for Caen to the east. "No power in the world," Hitler had boasted, "can drive us out of this region," but within five days the Allies had landed sixteen divisions in France. A month later they broke through the German lines defending Paris, and on August 24, Paris was liberated. No wonder Stalin could cable, "The history of wars does not know any such undertaking, so broad in conception, so grandiose in scale, and so masterly in execution."

By December 1944 it was clear that Germany was defeated. Italy had been knocked out of the war; the Russians were hammering at Germany's eastern frontiers; the Allies had driven from Normandy to Paris, and from Paris to Belgium and the Rhine; General Patton's armies had liberated southern France; and Allied bombers were reducing many German cities to rubble. Faced with disaster, Hitler determined on a desperate gamble for victory: to assemble a new army and air force, break through the American lines in the Ardennes, smash through to Antwerp, and disrupt the whole supply system of the Allied powers. Because bad weather prevented air reconnaissance, von Rundstedt's army achieved complete surprise when, on December 16, 1944, they broke the 106th Division in the Ardennes and thrust towards the Meuse. They were everywhere successful, except at Bastogne where a small United States force held out desperately against the advance.

The Battle of the Bulge, from December 16 to 26, became one of the heroic episodes in American military history. On the 17th, the 101st Airborne, then on rest leave in Paris, drove all night with headlights blazing and reached Bastogne the next morning in time to save the little garrison from disaster. Then followed one of the fiercest battles of the war. For six days the Germans hurled armor and planes at the defenders, while foul weather prevented Allied aerial support. When on the 22nd the Germans made a formal demand for surrender, General McAuliffe of the 101st Airborne gave the simple answer, "Nuts!" Next day the weather cleared and planes began dropping supplies. Meantime General Patton's Third Army started pell-mell north to the rescue; on December 26th, his 4th Armored Division

TANK COMMANDER.
c. 1963. Opaque watercolor, 16½x15¾ in. Collection Mr. Roy Lawrence.

broke through the German lines. Bastogne was saved. Within a few weeks the original lines had been restored. Rundstedt's gamble had failed at a cost of 120,000 men, 1,600 planes, and most of his tanks.

Though it was the Japanese attack on Pearl Harbor that precipitated the entry of the United States into World War II, Roosevelt and Marshall wisely decided that the war against Hitler—who seemed on the verge of triumph—must take priority over the war in the Pacific. Because of the initial damage to the navy at Pearl Harbor, and because of the huge distances involved, the Pacific War was, at first, a series of setbacks. The tide of battle turned on June 4, 1942, when Admirals Spruance and Fletcher inflicted the first naval defeat ever suffered by Japan in her history at the Battle of Midway.

On December 3, 1943, the Combined Chiefs to Staff agreed on the basic strategy for the Pacific War: "to obtain bases from which the unconditional surrender of Japan can be forced." After the Battle of Midway, it was possible for the rebuilt American navy and air force to take the offensive. General MacArthur wished to liberate the Philippines first and then move on from there to Formosa and the

**THE MONEY GAME. 1957.
Mixed media, 12x25 in.
Collection United States
Secret Service, Washington,
D.C.
"I recently reworked some
of this painting so that it
could be made into a
limited edition print for the
Secret Service."**

China coast, and from these vantage points hammer Japan into submission; the navy preferred island-hopping. By capturing much of the northern Chinese coast, the Japanese eliminated the first alternative, and at a historic meeting in Hawaii on July 14, 1944, President Roosevelt, General Mac-Arthur, and Admiral Nimitz agreed on the reconquest of the Philippines. In accordance with carefully worked out plans, the Americans landed over one hundred thousand men on the shores of Leyte Gulf on the 20th of October. "I have returned," said General MacArthur. "Rally to me. Let no heart be faint." Of necessity the Japanese moved in to destroy the out-numbered American naval forces.

The Battle of Leyte Gulf, October 20–25th, was, says Admiral Morison, "the greatest naval battle of all time" —and the greatest naval victory, too. The Japanese navy never thereafter recovered. It was during this battle that the Japanese first resorted to suicide, or "kamikaze," attacks on American ships. The word "kamikaze" means "heavenly wind" and was the name given to a typhoon which, centuries earlier, had driven hostile Chinese ships from Japanese shores. Doubtless, the Japanese were hoping once again for such divine intervention. As the Japanese navy was slowly bled to death, it relied increasingly on these suicide attacks to cripple American warships. The new tactic was used with considerable effect, most notably in the prolonged struggle for Okinawa (April 1–June 22, 1945) where kamikaze pilots took a toll of twenty-nine ships sunk and some sixty others put out of service.

B.B. WASHINGTON UNDER ATTACK. 1970. Oil on illustration board, 24x15¾ in. Collection Mr. Harry Glass.

Right:
KAMIKAZE ATTACK ON THE SARATOGA. 1963. Opaque watercolor, 12⅛x18¾ in. Collection United States Navy Memorial Museum, Washington, D.C.

194

ATTACK AT SEA. 1971.
Oil on illustration board,
25x14¾ in. Collection of
Mr. Harry Glass.

The Japanese ambition for conquest and for empire exceeded even that of Hitler. The invasion of China in the late 1930s was merely the first step in a plan for conquering half the world. That plan looked eastward to the conquest of the Philippines and, perhaps, of Hawaii; southward for some four thousand miles to dominion over the vast archipelago that stretched from Malaya to Java and New Britain, and, eventually, to Australia; and westward to dominion over Indochina, Burma, and India. Within Japan's grasp—so her deluded leaders thought—lay the greatest empire in all history.

The job that faced Roosevelt after the disaster at Pearl Harbor was to save Hawaii and recover the Philippines; the job that faced Churchill, after the fall of Singapore, with its eighty thousand defenders—the worst defeat Britain had ever suffered—was to protect Australia and India. In January of 1942 Roosevelt appointed the man who knew more about China than anyone else, General "Vinegar Joe" Stilwell, to command the American, British, and Chinese forces in Burma and China. His immediate task was to resist the Japanese advance towards India; and then to reopen the famed Burma Road, China's only lifeline to the outside world.

With meagre forces and inadequate air or weapon power, and without the support of Chiang Kai-Shek—who was much more concerned with fighting Chinese communists than Japanese invaders—Stilwell fought a masterly

RESCUE AT PANTAGIAN PRISON. 1958. Opaque watercolor, 15½x25⅛ in. Collection of the artist.

holding operation in the jungles of Burma for two years.
Then in the spring of 1944 he opened the Burma Road and
seized the offensive against the Japanese. He was never to
complete that offensive. At the insistence of Chiang—who
Stilwell early recognized as a broken reed, foreseeing that
Washington would best serve her own interests, and those
of China, by working with the communists—Stilwell was
recalled to the United States.

In an age of mechanized warfare, when commanders
are more often at headquarters, well behind the enemy lines,
dealing with large problems of logistics and strategy, a fighting general like Joseph Stilwell, who marched and fought
with his troops, inevitably takes on a special glamour.

Thereafter, the Americans took the offensive. The heroic contests for Guadalcanal, the Solomons, the Marianas, and the battles of the Philippine Sea and Leyte Gulf testify to their success. By early 1945 the Allies were ready to move against the Japanese mainland. Island after island had been taken, providing the strategic bases necessary for the final assault. This preparation for the conquest of Japan culminated with the taking of Iwo Jima, February 19, 1945. Three days later they reached the top of Mount Suribachi. For Americans it symbolized victory; for the Japanese, the beginning of the end. Yet it should be remembered that the taking of Mount Suribachi was not the taking of the island. The Americans had to fight on, their advance steady, but slow and bloody, until finally, on March 17, the island was theirs. Estimated casualties for the marines and navy totaled some seven thousand men—a high cost even for "conquest" of a small, desolate piece of rock that excited no man's interest in time of peace.

At the Cairo Conference of 1943, the Allied leaders pledged, "in due course Korea shall become free and independent." Russia's last-minute entry into the war against Japan—it came on August 9, 1945—enabled her to move troops into the Korean Peninsula, and at the surrender negotiations Korea was divided into zones of occupation—United States and Russian—at the 38th parallel. That did not, at the time, seem alarming, and when, in January 1950, Secretary Acheson outlined a "defensive perimeter" vital to our security, he did not include either Formosa or Korea. Just five months after that speech, North Korea invaded the South. The United Nations denounced the invasion and called on its members to resist it. Truman reacted instantly by ordering American ships and troops to Korea. For almost two months the North Koreans had things all their own way; but by mid-September General MacArthur had seized the offensive, recaptured Seoul, and stormed across the 38th parallel on the way to the northern border at the Yalu River. China responded by massing troops on the Yalu and, late in November, unleashing a ferocious counterattack, sent the United States forces reeling back across the 38th parallel.

That winter saw some of the cruelest warfare in American history—a treacherous terrain and a ferocious en-

KOREAN WINTER.
c. 1958. Opaque watercolor, 16x14¾ in. Collection Mrs. R. Brandon.

Right:
COWBOY ARTILLERY AT SOYANG. 1983. Oil on canvas, 24x32 in. Collection National Guard Bureau, Pentagon.
"The 300th AFA Battalion from Wyoming in an action during May of 1951 made an heroic and determined stand that earned them a Presidential Unit Citation. I worked with historians from the National Guard in order to recreate this scene as accurately as possible. Later I was thrilled to receive a letter from Adjutant General James L. Spence of the Wyoming National Guard commending me on my efforts. He told me that Bill White, a crewman on the *Lucky Seven*, said my painting was 'perfect,' and added, 'I couldn't have hoped for more. That's how it was.' I have never received a higher compliment or one that pleased me more."

emy equipped with Russian-made tanks and planes. When MacArthur threatened to bomb mainland China, Truman recalled him. Finally the United Nations forces came out on top in South Korea; and when the next June the Soviet Union suggested an armistice at the 38th parallel, Washington welcomed the proposal.

After the prolonged and acrimonious controversy over the New Deal and the welfare state, the all-embracing involvement in the "greatest of wars," the excitement of postwar settlements, and the emergence of the Cold War (dramatized by the war in Korea), the American mind—and temper—yearned for quiet and even for escape. President Eisenhower, who had earned his credentials as a central figure in war, nevertheless seemed to satisfy that yearning; in retrospect, the Eisenhower years are remembered as an interlude of peace in a long era of turbulence. All this was, to be sure, deceptive—and escapist. The problems were there, glaring upon us from every quarter of the horizon: the Cold War, the threat of atomic war, the rapid exhaustion of natural resources, the deterioration of the cities, the upsurge of racial violence and crime—all problems that would come home to roost, as it were, in the 1960s.

The 1950s hosted a society which rather smugly thought itself successful and could, therefore, afford to indulge the young in ostentatious displays of youthfulness. Almost everyone, in that age, went to high school; and soon many would be going to college as well. High school and college were designed, in theory at least, for the pursuit of learning. In the eyes of the average American, however, the deity of both high school and college was that of Dionysius, not of Apollo. As, in the United States, it was taken for granted that most students would have, or have access to cars, these high-spirited youngsters are shown in a Model-A Ford, doubtless of early vintage. They are celebrating an athletic victory over some rival—in all likelihood football, rather than basketball, for football was played in the afternoon and basketball (in defiance of the laws covering child labor) mostly at night. A very American painting, this, for passionate and overriding devotion to sports is an idiosyncrasy of American education.

**THAT WAS THE DAY.
1976. Oil on board, 24x32 in. Collection Mr. Harry Glass.**
"I came up with the idea for this painting when I saw this ferryboat in Mystic, Connecticut. My wife posed for two of the cheerleaders, so I named the boat after her."

Alone among the great powers that fought World War II, the United States emerged from that war with her industrial empire intact and her economy stronger than ever before in her history. She had escaped the ravages of invasion, which had cost the Soviet Union 25 million lives, and of mass bombing attacks that had destroyed most of the railroads, bridges, dams, and power plants and devastated most of the great cities of Europe. Inevitably, it was to the New World that a stricken Europe turned, in despair and in hope, to "step forth, once again, to the rescue and liberation of the Old." America's response was the Marshall Plan, which Winston Churchill called the "most unsordid act in history": a program that poured billions of dollars and mountains of food and machinery into her former Allies and—under a different authority—extended the same aid to rebuild Germany and Japan.

Happily, the United States was able to shoulder this unprecedented burden without difficulty. The war had not only left the American economy unimpaired, it had actually improved its efficiency and accelerated its growth. The 11 million members of the armed forces were quickly absorbed into the civilian economy; factories and industries were reconverted to civilian needs; agricultural production boomed; improved technology and new sources of energy were exploited; and limitless markets beckoned to both private and public enterprise.

In the generation after the war, national production increased from $200 to over $700 billion a year, oil production soared by 200 percent, and electrical energy increased no less than eightyfold. New York became the financial center of the world; American farms fed tens of millions throughout the globe; her airplanes touched down at every airport; her banks financed business and industry on every continent. What is more, American universities and technological institutes attracted scientists from every civilized country. In 1969, that leadership was dramatized by the landing of the first men on the moon, and it has been confirmed over the years by the award to American scientists (many of them, to be sure, refugees from other lands) of thirty-nine Nobel Prizes in medicine, thirty-eight in physics, and twenty in chemistry.

Top:
OIL WELLS. 1983. Mixed media, 15½x13½ in. Collection United States Steel.

Above:
COMPUTERIZED STEEL. 1983. Mixed media, 15½x13½ in. Collection of the artist.

Right:
NO JOB TOO TOUGH. 1974. Oil on illustration board, 16x16 in. Collection of the artist.
"Again neighbors posed for all the workers, except for the mean-looking one at the far right—that was a self-portrait."

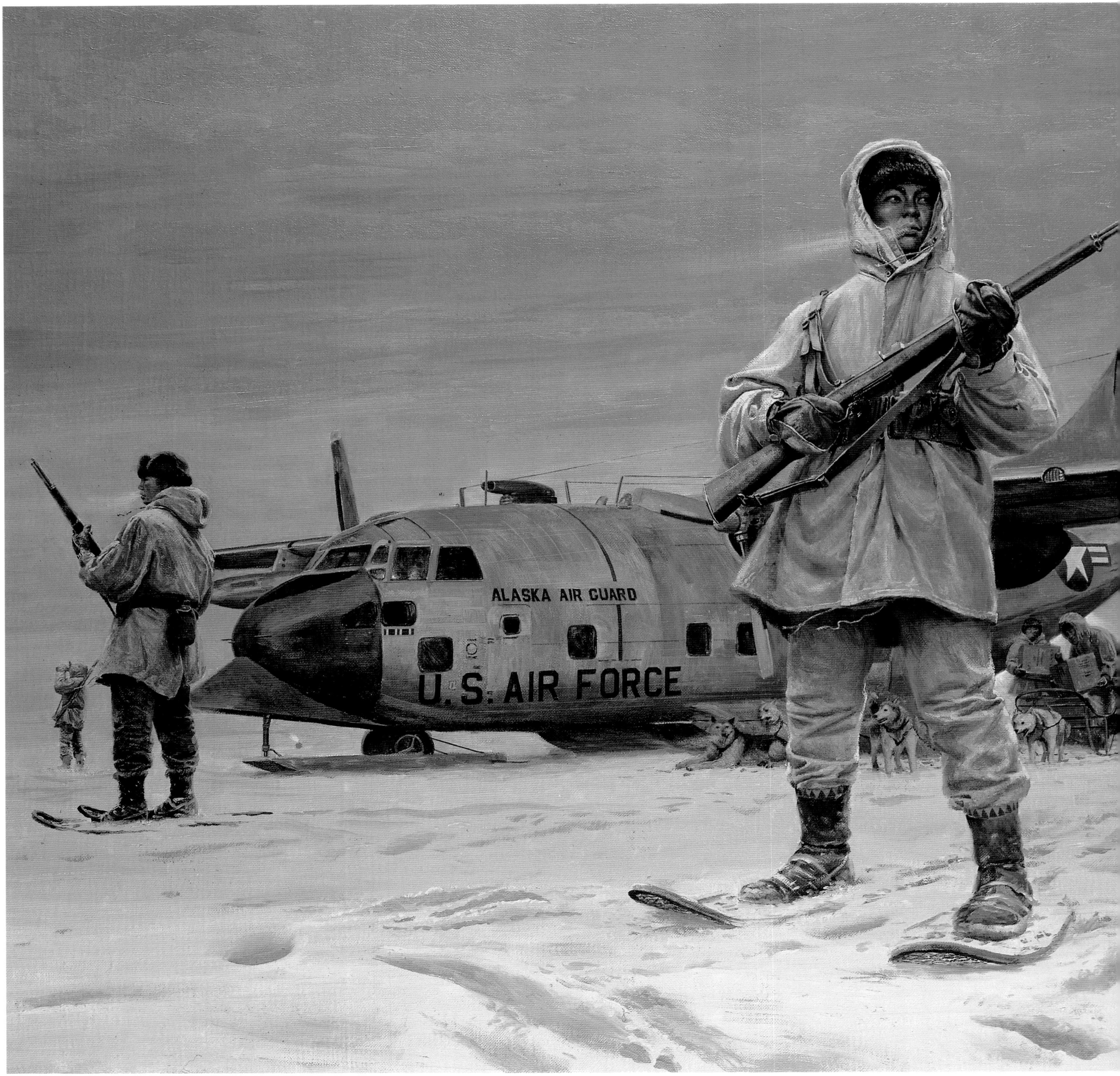
ALASKA AIR GUARD
U.S. AIR FORCE

Fear of and hostility to communism were nothing new in the postwar years. It was born of the Communist Revolution of 1917—after all, not until 1933 did the United States recognize the Soviet Union. The overriding need to defeat Nazi Germany dictated an alliance between Britain, the United States, and the Soviet Union, but even before the war was over the old antagonism between these nations flared up again. What might be regarded as an infor-

Left:
GUARDIANS OF THE NORTH. 1984. Oil on canvas, 24x32 in. Collection National Guard Bureau, Pentagon.
"These Eskimo scouts from the 297th Infantry of the Alaska National Guard are seen receiving supplies on the frozen tundra during the winter of 1968."

Right, top:
RAMEY AIR FORCE BASE, PUERTO RICO—CUTTING SUGAR CANE. 1958. Oil on canvas, 24x48 in. Collection United States Air Force Museum, Boulder, Colorado.

Right, bottom:
RAMEY AIR FORCE BASE—THE COLD WAR. 1958. Oil on canvas, 30x40 in. Collection United States Air Force Museum, Boulder, Colorado.

mal declaration of Cold War came in March of 1946 with Winston Churchill's famous address at Fulton, Missouri, where he asserted that "from the Baltic to the Adriatic an Iron Curtain has descended across the Continent" and called for the United States to take the lead in destroying it. With the Soviet blockade of Berlin in 1947, and the almost miraculous success of the Anglo-American Berlin Airlift, the Cold War was formally on. It persisted until 1989, expanding to embrace Soviet satellites and China and contracting when these moved towards greater independence—not from communism, but from the Soviet Union. It plunged the two most powerful nations on the globe into an insensate arms race, each pouring tens of billions of dollars each year into new armaments, mostly nuclear. Again and again there was a threat that the Cold War might become a hot war. That catastrophe, which would spell destruction for a good part of mankind, was avoided.

The Cold War affected many countries, but probably none more profoundly than the United States herself. It called into existence a national security state, helped build up a military-industrial-labor-finance-science-university complex, and dictated intervention in the internal affairs of a score of nations throughout the world.

Not every manifestation of this outburst of energy and enterprise spelled "progress," or even prosperity. Far from all Americans share equally in its rewards. Thus the "revolution" in agriculture made it possible for 4 million farmers to produce what 15 million had produced in an earlier generation. The new agriculture not only drove farmers into the cities, it mined the soil and made dangerous demands on water. Jefferson's dream of an idyllic rural republic faded away. Nor were the rewards of industry and finance equitably distributed during the generation after the war. The rich grew richer and the poor grew poorer, and the number of those unable to manage in an economy that required special skills, mounted. By the 1980s, an official survey discovered some 20 million citizens without enough food to satisfy their hunger.

The physical plant, too, deteriorated. Railroads were abandoned and, as transportation by automobiles and airplanes used up the petroleum resources of the nation, the costs

CLOUDY AND COLDER. 1977. Oil on illustration board, 16½x12½ in. Collection Mr. Howard Weingrow. "Literally done overnight, this painting was used as the cover for the April 11, 1977, issue of the international edition of *Newsweek.*"

Right: **ASPIRATIONS.** 1970. Oil on board, 19x26 in. Collection Westvaco. "Debbi and my son David posed here for the mother and son. The model for the father was Lew Hollaway, an artist friend."

saddled on future generations rose. Industry moved to the Sun Belt and, as in earlier years when millions of blacks moved from an impoverished South to a prosperous North, now millions of Hispanics from Mexico and the Caribbean countries sought a new Promised Land. With rising costs the richest nation in the world found herself with an ever-mounting debt, and unable to provide for the health and welfare of the victims of the new economy. For the first time in history, what had been a model of equality found itself confronted with the threat of a class society.

Partly as a consequence of the victorious war in the Pacific, and their subsequent responsibility for a conquered Japan, Americans persuaded themselves that the United States was not only a Pacific, but an Asian power. With the triumph of Mao Tse-Tung over Chiang Kai-Shek, American paranoia about communism was enlarged to embrace Asia as well as Europe. Thus, when the forces of Ho Chi Minh finally defeated the French effort to restore colonialism in Indochina at Dien Bien Phu (May of 1954), the United States was already committed to a free, non-communist Vietnam. The French forces, during their last years in Indochina, had been supported financially, in large part, by American military aid. That aid continued to flow to their anti-communist successors. Eisenhower avoided direct intervention, but President Kennedy dispatched some fourteen thousand military "advisors" to help the existing government. President Johnson, after his election in 1964, escalated "intervention" into a full-scale war.

The Vietnam War lasted over ten years—longer than any other war in American history. It exacted a toll of over 250,000 American casualties and of perhaps one and one-half million Vietnamese and Cambodians. It shattered the fabric of social and economic life in Vietnam and all but destroyed the country by bombing. It cost hundreds of billions of dollars in direct military expenditures and equal sums in the distraction of the economy and research to nonproductive purposes. It tore American society apart, exacerbated corruption in government, contributed to the degradation of politics, weakened the constitutional system, and forfeited the good opinion of much of the civilized world. It was, in short, after slavery, the most tragic chapter of American history.

VIETNAM PROTEST. c. 1965. Opaque watercolor, 16x14¾ in. Collection Mr. and Mrs. Jack Fuchs.

Right:
INDIANA RANGERS: THE ARMY GUARD IN VIETNAM. 1984. Oil on canvas, 24x32 in. Collection National Guard Bureau, Pentagon.
"This Ranger patrol, Company D, 151st Infantry, is on a reconnaissance and intelligence-gathering mission. Delta Company achieved an impressive combat record; its members were awarded 510 medals for valor and service."

These calamities cannot be charged against the fighting men; they were, as truly as the Vietnamese, victims of the war. The rank and file in all services fought with courage and loyalty as have soldiers in most wars. Mr. Künstler has given us here a glimpse of what war was like in the jungles of South Vietnam.

How can the propensity of Americans to violence and crime be explained? First, the settlement of America was the unsettlement of those who left Europe or Africa for America. They tore up their roots, and left behind their customs, laws, religious and legal commitments that had, for centuries, provided the boundaries of their lives. Second, life in the New World invited—at times almost required—violence and lawlessness: the open land was had for the taking; Indians were regarded as savages with no real rights to the soil, who were to be driven out or killed off; slavery, in the word of Thomas Jefferson, "a perpetual exercise of the most boisterous of passions, "all too often degraded master and slave alike. Add to this a philosophy of individualism—originally a perjorative term—which not only invited but rewarded self-aggrandizement and the exploitation of the weak, in a ceaseless quest for wealth and power, and a violent exploitation of nature, an exploitation that still goes on before our eyes. As Tocqueville observed back in the 1830s, an equalitarian democracy is peculiarly susceptible to the temptations of taking a quick and easy road to success, and, when these expectations are frustrated, finds it easy to follow a tortuous rather than a straight and narrow path. There is a final and sobering consideration: the very government responsible for preventing violence, is, by its military solutions to problems throughout the globe and by its reliance on force instead of diplomacy, itself setting an example that is not lost upon its citizens. As Justice Brandeis put it "the potent, the omnipresent teacher. . . . It teaches the whole people by its example. Crime is contagious. If the government becomes a law breaker it breeds contempt for law. It invites every man to become a law unto himself. It invites anarchy."

THE GUARDS. 1974.
Gouache, 12x12 in.
Collection Buffalo Savings
Bank, Buffalo, New York.

Right:
THE CAPER. 1970. Oil on
illustration board, 22x16 in.
Collection Mr. S. Brozman.

212

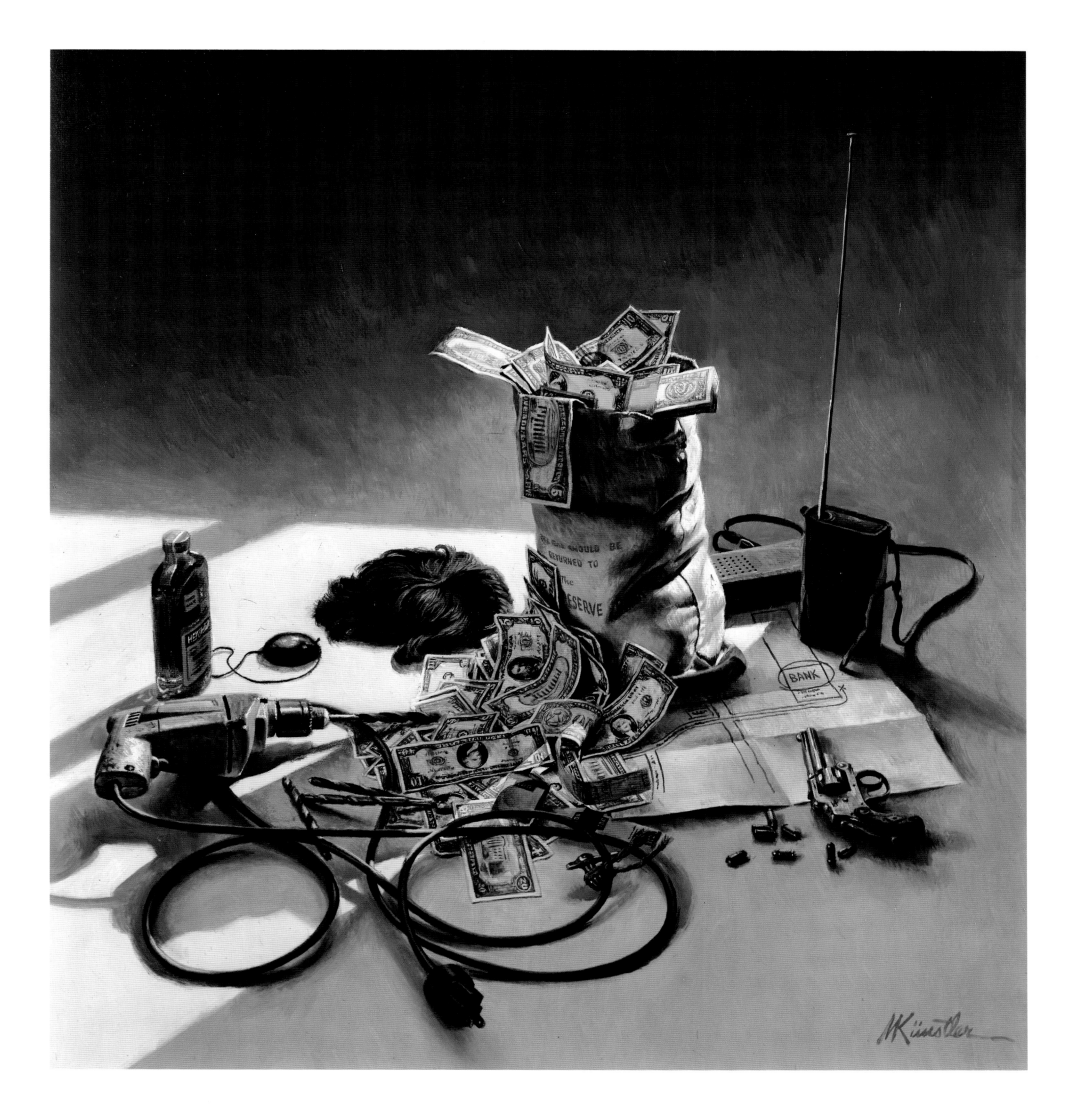

IX. The Space Age

IX. THE SPACE AGE

The dream of penetrating outer space and exploring the moon is as old as mankind. It was what Icarus aimed for and has been the subject of countless romances from the second century on through to the twentieth. It remained for Americans—in cooperation to be sure with scientists of other countries—to achieve the dream.

During World War II, the Germans had turned away from atomic weaponry and fixed their hopes on rockets instead. Accordingly, they established rocket sites along the north German coasts, from which they assaulted Britain. The Allies captured these sites, and with them the rocket experts: many of them were brought to the United States to direct our program in rockets. Now ensued a race for the conquest of outer space. In 1957, the Soviets won the first leg of that race, as it were, by successfully launching *Sputnik I* and *II*, which orbited the earth every 103 minutes. Taking up the gauntlet, in 1961 President Kennedy declared, "I believe that we should go to the moon before this decade is out," and persuaded Congress to support an intensive space program. It was Kennedy who named the program *Apollo*.

Page 215:
LAUNCH OF THE SPACE SHUTTLE COLUMBIA (Detail).

JOHN GLENN AND FRIENDSHIP 7. 1985. Opaque watercolor, 12x14 in. Collection Fleetwood, Division of Unicover Corp., Cheyenne, Wyoming.

Right:
LANDING ON THE MOON. 1984. Opaque watercolor, 12x14 in. Collection Fleetwood, Division of Unicover Corp., Cheyenne, Wyoming.

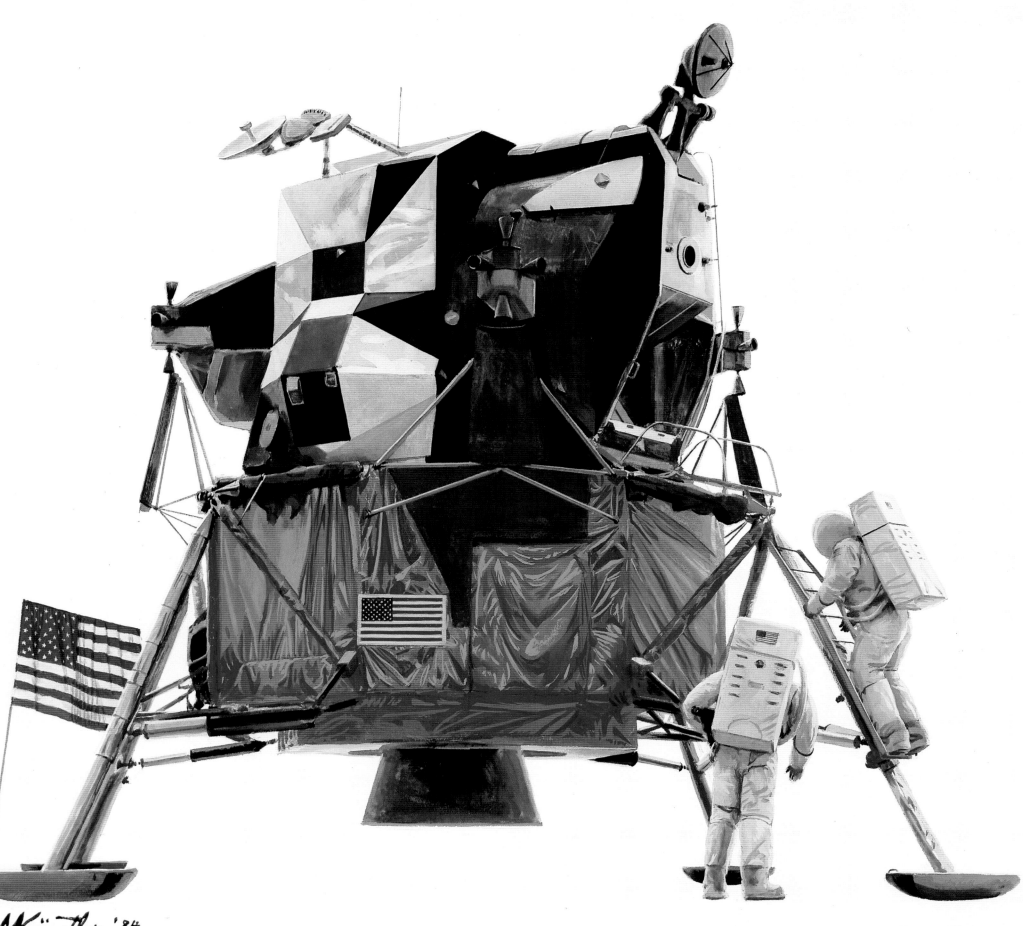

218

After some years of preliminary explorations, we began the final Apollo experiments. The summer of 1969, the astronauts were ready for the decisive test; and on July 16, *Apollo II*—named the *Eagle*—blasted off from Cape Kennedy on its historic mission. Four days later, at 4:17 in the afternoon, Neil Armstrong and Edwin Aldrin, Jr., landed a lunar module on the moon, becoming the first men ever to walk on its surface. "That's one small step for man, one giant step for mankind," said Armstrong; then he set up a plaque with the inscription "Here men from the planet Earth first set foot upon the moon. We came in peace for all mankind." Armstrong's father had suggested a different, perhaps, more fitting inscription taken from the Psalms: "When we behold the heavens, the work of Your fingers, the moon and the stars which You set in place, what is man that You should be mindful of him."

For many years now scientists have been working toward fulfilling the dreams of fiction writers who, unhampered by the law of gravity or the tremendous heat generated by re-entry into the earth's atmosphere, routinely sent men traveling to and fro in space to settle the "Final Frontier." With the successful launching of the ninety-ton *Columbia* in 1981, fact moved closer to fiction. Although it will still be a long while before the space stations familiar to Flash Gordon and Star Trek fans are built, the advent of a manned, reusable spacecraft, capable of carrying large quantities of materials in its sixty-foot-long cargo bay, means that such dreams are no longer mere fantasy.

It was on April 12 at 7:00 A.M. (exactly twenty years after Soviet cosmonaut, Yuri Gagarin, became the first man to orbit the earth) that the space shuttle *Columbia* was launched from Cape Canaveral, the huge rocket engines consuming some 1 million pounds of propellant as they hurtled the immense craft into space. Thus began the 54½-hour orbit of seasoned astronauts John Young and Robert Crippen; thus the doors to the "Final Frontier" finally opened wide.

Plans for such a vehicle had been on the drawingboard ever since young navy test pilots first began breaking the sound barrier some thirty years earlier. However, the space shuttle program would be delayed until the Soviet Union successfully launched *Sputnik I* in 1957. The Soviets had a man in space; the rockets needed to launch a craft

FLAG ON THE MOON.
1977. Oil on board,
15¾x19¾ in. Collection Mr.
Homer Noble.
"With this painting and the one preceding it I had to confront the problem of over-familiarity. Most people know the scene very well from the outstanding photographs and news coverage that surrounded the moon landing. By showing both astronauts at once I eliminated any similarity to the photographs of the period while I presented a new and different viewpoint."

Sketch:
FIRST ROLLOUT OF ENTERPRISE.
Oil on paper.

Left:
FIRST ROLLOUT OF ENTERPRISE, 17 SEPTEMBER 1976, PALMDALE, CALIFORNIA. 1980. Oil on canvas, 40x54 in. Collection Rockwell International Corp. "After I received the commission to document the space shuttle I became totally involved in the program and saw the hangar at Palmdale and the *Enterprise* up close. This painting is a reconstruction of the rollout; I did not witness the actual event. After seeing the many photographs taken on that historic day, however, I noticed that none had been taken from inside the hangar, and immediately decided upon that as the perspective of my painting."

like *Columbia*, and her sister ships *Challenger* and *Discovery* were not yet developed, and would take too long to begin operating. As the United States joined the Soviet Union's "race to the moon," attention focused upon the smaller and more costly (because they were not reusable) but more feasible vehicles such as those used in the Apollo and Gemini projects.

Although it will still be a long time before a "Space Family Robinson" actually exists, or before travel to and from space will be considered nothing out of the ordinary, *Columbia* pointed the way, and it, and the other shuttles, will continue to do so as they orbit the earth, retrieve heretofore irretrievable communication satellites and undergo fantastic test and operational flights. Work stations, space laboratories, industries located in the vast reaches of outer space might well strain our imagination. The successful launching, however, of the somewhat graceless *Columbia*, nicknamed "Dumbo, the Space Truck" by the irreverent, from Cape Canaveral in 1981; its exciting re-entry into the earth's atmosphere through heat measuring some two thousand degrees; and its eventual "gliding home" to Edwards Air Force Base in California would have strained the imagination of even the wildly imaginative Jules Verne. Whether or not the benefits to humankind will balance out the hundreds of billions of dollars required to fulfill the scientific and literary dreams remains to be seen.

APPLICATION OF THE
HEAT SHIELD TILES,
6 MAY 1980, JOHN F.
KENNEDY SPACE CENTER,
FLORIDA. 1980. Oil
on canvas, 30x23 in.
Collection Rockwell
International Corp.

Left:
ROCKWELL TILE TEAM,
6 MAY 1980, JOHN F.
KENNEDY SPACE CENTER,
FLORIDA. 1980. Oil
on canvas, 26x36 in.
Collection Rockwell
International Corp.
"On first walking into the
hangar, I experienced a very
strange feeling. It was
almost impossible to tell
there was a space craft
above me."

TILE TEAM. 6 MAY 1980.
JOHN F. KENNEDY SPACE
CENTER, FLORIDA.
1980. Oil on canvas,
26½x20½ in. Collection
NASA, Washington, D.C.
"At the Kennedy Space
Center I found people from
all walks of life working
as hard as they could to do
the best job possible. Each
one felt the lives of the
astronauts were in his
hands."

TEST FIRING THE MAIN ENGINE, 12 JULY 1980, NATIONAL SPACE TECHNOLOGY LABORATORIES, BAY ST. LOUIS, MISSISSIPPI. 1980.
Oil on canvas, 40x30 in.
Collection Rockwell International Corp.
"It is blistering hot in Mississippi in the middle of July, and when the engine fired I thought that if the heat did not get me, the sound would. The noise was almost deafening, even though I was standing several miles away."

ENGLE AND TRULY. 1981.
Oil on canvas, 15x12 in.
Collection Mr. John Oscher.
"After buying the portrait of
Crippen and Young, John
Oscher commissioned me to
do this painting of Joe
Engle and Dick Truly, the
second flight crew of the
space shuttle, as a mate, and
Engle and Truly were kind
enough to pose for me."

CRIPPEN AND YOUNG.
1981. Oil on canvas, 15x12
in. Collection Mr. John
Oscher.
"When I first met Bob
Crippen and John Young in
Houston they were
surrounded by hundreds of
photographers and reporters
from all over the world.
Although almost every
minute of their day was
spoken for, they took the
time to pose for me. Later,
when they had more time I
met them again, this time at
NASA in Washington."

Sketches:
LAUNCH OF SPACE
SHUTTLE COLUMBIA.

Right:
LAUNCH OF SPACE
SHUTTLE COLUMBIA,
12 APRIL 1981, 7:00:10 EST,
JOHN F. KENNEDY SPACE
CENTER, FLORIDA. 1981.
Oil on canvas, 60x40 in.
Collection Rockwell
International Corp.
"The tension surrounding
the launch of this space
shuttle was enormous. At
launch, the five engines
were fired simultaneously,
creating a thrust of almost
seven million pounds. First
a huge cloud of smoke shot
up from the launch pad,
then the flames, brighter
than the sun. It took a few
seconds for the sound
to reach us, but when
it did it was absolutely
overwhelming. It felt like
an earthquake—the ground
even trembled—and we were
more than two miles away!
Altogether, it was an
incredible moment, one of
the most exciting experiences
of my life."

227

Sketches:
TOUCHDOWN OF SPACE SHUTTLE COLUMBIA. Oil on paper.

Right:
TOUCHDOWN OF SPACE SHUTTLE COLUMBIA, 14 APRIL 1981, 10:20:53 PST, EDWARDS AFB, CALIFORNIA. 1981. Oil on canvas, 40x54 in. Collection Rockwell International Corp.
"It seems that people who witness their first shuttle launch have one of two reactions: either they look aghast and say, 'Oh my God!' or they cry. At the touchdown, everyone cheered. We had to wait for four hours in the desert heat of Edwards Air Force Base, but hearing astronauts Bob Crippen and John Young describe what it was like 'up there' made it all worthwhile."

EPILOGUE   By Rod Gragg

Like a mighty river, the American spirit flowed across the land. Through vast woodlands, over mountain passes, across prairielands and deserts it surged. Down the Merrimac, the Mississippi, and the Missouri; up the Congaree, the Colorado, and the Columbia it spread. By masted ships, ox cart, mule team, Conestoga, stagecoach, flatboat, keelboat, steamboat, and narrow gauge rail it moved. Over the Wilderness Road, the Oregon Trail, the Natchez Trace, the Santa Fe Trail, the Texas Road, and Round-the-Horn it travelled. It labored past lyrical-sounding landmarks like Great Falls and Crown Point, Split Rock, and Grandfather Mountain, Beartooth Pass and the Painted Desert, Mount of the Holy Cross and the Graveyard of the Atlantic. Onward—ever onward—it spread, from Key West to Skagway, from Acadia Bay to Diamond Head.

It was Booker T. Washington, up from slavery, and Theodore Roosevelt, up San Juan Hill. It was Nathan Hale's one life and Neil Armstrong's one small step. It was the dedicated leadership of George Washington, the character of Robert E. Lee, and the ingenuity of Sequoia.

It was the humility of George Washington Carver, the genius of Bernard Baruch, the adventurous drive of Daniel Boone, and the faith of Jonathan Edwards. It was the selflessness of Clara Barton, the whimsical wit of Will Rogers, and the discipline of Stonewall Jackson. It was the talent of Aaron Copeland, the daring of Charles Lindberg, and the determination of Joshua Lawrence Chamberlain.

It is the best of a people—it is the American spirit.

And at its best it springs ever fresh from its origins as a nation of laws, not men—the world's oldest surviving democratic republic—founded on the simple, profound principle of "one nation under God." The Declaration of Independence was a people's statement of intent based on an essential and fundamental perspective: "We hold these Truths to be self-evident," the founding document proclaimed, "that all men are created equal, that they are endowed by their Creator with certain unalienable Rights, that among these are Life, Liberty, and the Pursuit of Happiness."

That foundational truth was the cement that bonded the United States of America through war and peace, prosperity and privation, hard times and good times. It was issued that July 4, 1776, as a patriot's dream by men who solemnly realized its simple proclamation endangered their lives.

Such a principle was the unique expression of Judeo-Christian values, the fulfillment of Western civilization, and a two-edged sword

WE, THE PEOPLE . . . 1787.
1986. Oil on canvas, 30x48 in.
Collection PICA Foundation,
Charlotte, North Carolina.

of liberty that severed the bonds of oppression forward through the ages and around the globe. Immediately, it bequeathed an equally fundamental principle of government. "That to secure these Rights, Governments are instituted among Men, deriving their just Powers from the Consent of the Governed." Government should be "just," this declaration proclaimed, limited in power and controlled in application by the "consent" of those it governed.

The signers ended their Declaration with a vow: "And for the support of this Declaration, with a firm Reliance on the Protection of divine Providence, we mutually pledge to each other our Lives, our Fortunes, and our sacred Honor." Lives. Fortunes. Honor. In the decades that have followed that patriotic vow, in places close and far away, on fields of sorrow and glory with names like Valley Forge and Lundy's Lane, Chancellorsville and Belleau Wood, Tarawa and Omaha Beach, legions of Americans have sacrificed lives, fortunes, and honor to preserve those "unalienable Rights . . . endowed by their Creator."

What the Declaration of Independence proposed, the U.S. Constitution established as a national doctrine. The early Articles of Confederation that united the thirteen new states had led not to order but to disorder. The new nation floundered; interstate commerce was frustrated; rivalry and not cooperation arose among the states; and the fledgling republic was vulnerable to outside aggression. The

THE FIRST AMENDMENT.
1987. Oil on canvas, 30x48 in.
Collection PICA Foundation,
Charlotte, North Carolina.

republic would survive and flourish, many of the Founding Fathers believed, only if the principles of the Declaration of Independence became the official doctrine of a national constitution.

But the concept frightened some. Would the central government come to dominate the states? Would it evolve into a weapon against the individual citizen? Would it be misused to strip away those "unalienable rights" granted to all by their Creator? Would state participation be voluntary? A national union too loose would only produce more chaos. A central government too powerful could result in tyranny. Too little democracy might produce oppression. Too much democracy could evolve into mob rule by a 51 percent majority.

On May 25, 1787, the Constitutional Convention held its first session in Philadelphia's Independence Hall. The first day, a bare majority of states was represented. Gradually, almost timidly, as if reluctant to empower a potentially fearsome central government, all the state delegates joined the great deliberation. The oldest was Benjamin Franklin, aged eighty-one. The youngest: New Jersey's twenty-six-year-old Jonathan Dayton. More than half the delegates were college educated. More than half were attorneys. Planters and merchants—and a few doctors and professors—composed the rest. Most prominent was George Washington, who was unanimously elected president of the convention. Driving the debate, most influential among deliberations, were seven men: George Mason and Edmund Randolph of Virginia, James Wilson and Governeur Morris of Pennsylvania, Connecticut's Roger Sherman, Elbridge Gerry of Massachusetts, and Virginia's James Madison.

On September 17, it was done. The document would have to be ratified by the states, but the delegates had produced the great document and it *would* be ratified. They had argued and cajoled, lobbied and deliberated, politicked and prayed. And what emerged was a foundational document of government unprecedented in history. Other governments had called themselves republics, but they had no safeguarding constitution like this one. Absent from this document were the self-centeredness of man, the arrogance, the evil, the excess of unrestrained democracy, the tyranny of unlimited political power. No king. No emperor. No mob rule. A government of checks and balances. A government, as one of the land's greatest leaders later described it, *of the people, by the people, and for the people.*

To hammer down that concept of limited government, the framers of the Constitution added ten amendments, the Bill of Rights. They forever clarified the intent of the Constitution to preserve and protect the principle freedoms of this democratic republic: freedom of religion, freedom of speech, freedom of the press, the right to assemble, the right of all to a speedy trial by jury, to bear arms for protection and defense, to have protection from unwarranted search and seizure, and to be spared cruel and unusual punishment. The ninth amendment was designed to protect citizens from any misuse of the Constitution itself, so that tyrants of the future could not wield the Constitution as a weapon to "deny or disparage others." And the tenth established a prohibition against a giant, swollen, and oppressive federal government so that the new national government would not be allowed to swallow up the state governments. "The powers not delegated to the United States by the Constitution, nor prohibited to it by the States, are reserved to the States respectively, or to the people." The national government should be checked, balanced, limited, confined to its proper role.

More than any other delegate, the title of "father" of the Constitution and the Bill of Rights belonged to Virginia's James Madison. "In framing a government which is to be administered by men over men," he observed, "the great difficulty lies in this: you must first enable the government to control the governed; and, in the next place, oblige it to control itself."

And that was what the incredible creation wrought by the delegates did, led greatly by Madison. He came to the Constitutional Convention better prepared to create a government than probably any other delegate. Short in stature at five-foot-six, he was a giant in ideas and an unmatched source of information on history, law, and political science. He addressed his fellow delegates 161 times. Persuasive, pushy, and stubborn, he benefited from the influence of older delegates, and his zeal and vision were channelled and disciplined into the architecture of an unprecedented creation: the Constitution of the United States of America.

How Madison must have felt when he held that document in his hands for the first time! Its seven articles were summarized in doctrinal form by the preamble: "We, the People of the United States, in order to form a more perfect union, establish justice, insure domestic tranquility, provide for the common defense, promote the general welfare, and secure the blessings of liberty to ourselves and our posterity, do ordain and establish this Constitution for the United States of America."

Like their predecessor—the Declaration of Independence—the Constitution and the Bill of Rights were the inheritors of the unique and lasting influence of Western civilization: the Judeo-Christian ethic that transferred to the American lawmakers the heritage of the higher law on which they based America's founding documents. At least fifty of the fifty-five men who framed the Constitution professed those traditional values. They had assembled in a unique time and place in history with a consensus upon which they forged a nation. Said Madison, "We have staked the whole future of the American civilization, not upon the power of the government, far from it. We have staked the future . . . upon the capacity of each and all of us to govern ourselves, to control ourselves, to sustain ourselves according to the Ten Commandments of God."

According to tradition, when the delegates emerged with their creation, a concerned woman inquired of Benjamin Franklin, "Well, Dr. Franklin. What have you given us?"

"You have a republic, madam," Franklin replied, "if you can keep it."

And through the ages it *has* been kept, fueled by the American spirit it ignited. It was not immune from error, from disharmony, from disaster, but the historic values of its founding documents, when faithfully followed, allowed it to endure, expand, and flourish from sea to shining sea. And what has emerged through the ages, awaiting preservation by the generations of today and tomorrow, is a wondrous and noble legacy—"one nation under God, indivisible, with liberty and justice for all."

BIOGRAPHY OF THE ARTIST
by M. Stephen Doherty

Mort Künstler is known as America's foremost historical artist, but over the course of his forty-year career he has achieved many other distinctions. His name is well known to the publishers of books and magazines and the art directors of advertising agencies because Künstler first made his mark as an outstanding illustrator. His paintings appeared on the covers of *Newsweek* and *Sports Afield*, in promotions for many motion pictures, and in countless advertisements and magazines.

Since 1977, when his paintings were first shown in major gallery and museum exhibitions, Künstler has been recognized as a fine artist. He has had nine one-man shows at the prestigious Hammer Galleries on Fifty-seventh Street in New York and numerous one-man exhibitions in museums around the country.

In recent years Künstler has become the most sought-after painter of American military history, with his prints, drawings, and oils of Civil War events enjoying a wide demand. This book is just one of several devoted to the varied and extensive collection of his paintings.

To understand how Künstler achieved this enviable status, we need to trace the artist's development from his earliest experiences to his latest paintings. In so doing, we will gain an even greater appreciation of Künstler's extraordinary talent.

A poster illustration that Künstler painted for the movie *The Poseidon Adventure*.

His parents, Tom and Rebecca Künstler, encouraged his interest in art even before he started school. "My father was an amateur artist," Mort recalls. "He gave me art supplies and drawing lessons before I entered PS 215 elementary school in Brooklyn. My mother was a schoolteacher, and she would take me to the museums by subway every Saturday morning."

Künstler also developed an interest in sports as a child, and even though he was small for his age, he had a natural talent for athletics. He was elected to his high school athletic honor society, graduated at the age of fifteen, and enrolled at Brooklyn College. His interest in art was second only to his love of sports, and Künstler eventually became the first four-letter man the college had ever had, competing against much older athletes. He subsequently was inducted into the school's sports hall of fame. The only artwork he did at the time was sports cartoons for the college newspaper.

After two years at Brooklyn College, Künstler went to UCLA on a basketball scholarship. While he was in California, his father suffered a heart attack, so he returned to Brooklyn to help care for him and enrolled at Pratt Institute. He continued to pursue his interests in art and basketball. During the summer he worked as a waiter and lifeguard at Tamarack Lodge in the Catskill Mountains and teamed up with future basketball great Bob Cousy to compete against players from the other resorts. "The resorts actively recruited outstanding athletes like Mort and me because each hotel had a team," Cousy remembers. "Mort and I were younger than most of the jocks who were playing basketball that summer. But both of us could handle ourselves well, and we held our own against some of the outstanding players who came up from New York City."

At the start of his senior year at Pratt, Künstler met his wife-to-be, Deborah, a freshman at the school. When he was graduated he worked for an illustration studio in New York. Deborah worked as a textile designer until their first child, David, was born. The couple bought a home on Long Island and converted half of the two-car garage into a studio. The family soon grew to five with daughters Amy and Jane.

Künstler's career as an illustrator began to take off in the late 1950s, even though the market had been reduced by the demise of several publications and the increased use of photographs in advertisements. His paintings appeared in some of the best-known publications of the day, including *True, Argosy, The Saturday Evening Post, Sports Afield, Outdoor Life,* and *Adventure*. In fact, business was so good that Künstler was almost overwhelmed by the amount of work he accepted. He and Debbi decided to move to Mexico for a few years so Mort could relax and spend more time with his family.

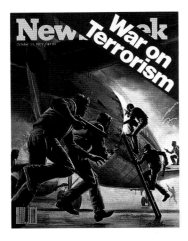

The illustration Künstler painted for the October 31, 1977, cover of the international edition of *Newsweek*.

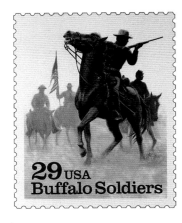

The U.S. Postal Service commissioned a painting of the Buffalo Soldiers from Künstler that was released as a stamp on April 22, 1994.

As much as the family enjoyed Mexico, they missed the excitement of New York. In 1963, the Künstlers returned to Long Island, and Mort began creating the kinds of historical paintings for which he is so well known today. Assignments from magazines like *National Geographic* and *Newsweek* and for movies such as *The Hindenburg* gave him a chance to research his subjects and use that information to compose dramatic depictions of important historic events.

His paintings also attracted the attention of gallery owners, private collectors, and museum directors. Through the 1970s, Künstler's artwork was exhibited at several galleries in New York, at the Daytona Beach Museum of Arts and Sciences in Daytona Beach, Florida, and at the Favell Museum in Klamath Falls, Oregon. In 1977, he had his first exhibit at Hammer Galleries and began a relationship that continues to this day.

In the late 1970s and early 1980s, Künstler's career continued to blossom, with major commissions from private collectors and corporations, more one-man shows with galleries, and the publication of books reproducing his paintings. In 1979, Abbeville Press published *Mort Künstler's 50 Epic Paintings of America*, with text by the distinguished American historian Henry Steele Commager. In 1981, Künstler was asked by Rockwell International Corporation to record the manufacture, testing, launch, and landing of the first space shuttle, *Columbia*. He travelled to California, Mississippi, Texas, and Florida to research this project, taking photographs and making sketches of scenes related to this historic event. Those drawings and paintings were exhibited for the first time at the Pittsburgh Center for the Arts in October 1981. The entire collection is now on permanent exhibition at the California Museum of Science and Technology in Los Angeles.

In 1984, Künstler was commissioned by the National Guard to portray Theodore Roosevelt and his Rough Riders charging up San Juan Hill. It was a particularly challenging commission because it meant that Künstler would be dealing with the subject of one of Frederic Remington's best-known paintings. "I had been doing some paintings for the National Guard as part of their ongoing series of historic events of the country's militia," Künstler explains. "But when I received a call from the Pentagon asking if I would do a painting of the famous charge up San Juan Hill, I got very excited. Here I am living less than a mile from T.R.'s home, Sagamore Hill. I know members of the Roosevelt family, and I have done action paintings during all of my career. If ever I was destined to do a painting, it was this one."

Künstler's thorough research discovered that many of the circumstances depicted in Remington's painting were not completely accurate. Accounts of the battle indicated that the terrain was rough and grassy, yet Remington's soldiers looked as though they were running a foot race across a freshly mowed lawn. None of those men were loading their rifles, and all the shooting was being done from a standing position. Soldiers of the time would have knelt to reload their rifles and probably would have shot from a crouching or lying position. "My challenge became one of creating a different and hopefully more accurate presentation of the events, and at the same time making a good picture," said Künstler. His version was very well received by both art critics and historians.

From 1985 to the present, there has been an explosion of interest in Künstler's work from television and movie producers, book publishers, art buyers, and military buffs. Several more books on his paintings have been published, including *The American Spirit: The Paintings of Mort Künstler* (Harry N. Abrams, 1986), *Images of the Civil War* (Gramercy Books, 1992), and *Gettysburg: The Paintings of Mort Künstler* (Turner Publishing, 1993). The Gettysburg book was published as a companion to the epic film *Gettysburg*.

Künstler has also been the subject of a number of television programs. In October 1993, the Arts & Entertainment network aired a one-hour program on "Time Machine" entitled *Images of the Civil War: The Paintings of Mort Künstler*, with Jack Perkins as narrator. It showed the artist in his studio with many of his Civil War paintings. There was also a great deal of media attention for a commission the artist received to recreate the Battle of Cedar Creek, a historic event that occurred in front of Belle Grove Plantation mansion in Cedar Creek, Virginia. Prints of Künstler's painting, *Shenandoah Sunrise*, were sold and helped raise $50,000 for Belle Grove and the Cedar Creek Battlefield Foundation.

Künstler has become one of the most successful artists in the field of limited-edition prints. American Publishing Group of Gettysburg, Pennsylvania, publishes his Civil War and military art prints. The Danbury Mint has produced several popular series of collector plates based on Künstler's work. This success in the active field of Civil War collectibles is particularly surprising considering that Künstler had only done a handful of Civil War paintings before 1988.

As he looks back on all of his accomplishments and tries to explain why he has always been known as a fast, dedicated, thorough artist, Künstler draws an analogy between himself and a player on a baseball team: "The attitude you need for success in sports is really the same attitude you need for success as an artist. I think of a ballplayer out in the field who sees a ball being hit in his general direction and starts sprinting toward it. He starts out thinking he doesn't have a chance in the world of actually catching the ball, but he runs as fast as he can so he'll be as close as possible. As he gets closer he starts to think he might actually have a chance. At the last second he leaps at the ball, and sometimes he catches it. That's how great catches are made. When the same kind of attitude is applied to art, great paintings are made. I've always tried to run a little harder and stretch a little farther to make the best pictures I can, and I think that many times I have succeeded."

INDEX

**Pages 239 and 240:
GOING FOR THE BIG BULL
(Detail)**